TRANSFORMATIONS

by Jim Wilson, Tom Stringfellow
and
Randy McWhorter

Transformations
(c) 2002, Dr. James L. Wilson, all rights reserved

Visit our websites at http://www.freshministy.org and
http://www.firstbaptistbevhills.org.

 Published by:
Willow City Press is a Cooperative Program
Ministry of the California Southern Baptist
Convention

In Cooperation With:

Parakeleo Ministries
P.O. Box 461
Beverly Hills, CA 90213

ISBN 0-9661778-5-1

Dewey Decimal Classification: 262.15

Table of Contents

Section I - Transformed Lives

Section II - Transformed Hearts

Section III - Transformed Witness

Dedication

This book is dedicated to Lori Ann Wilson, who proved that a person doesn't have to live a long time to live well and make a difference in the world.

Acknowledgments

This book would not exist without the cooperation of Bill Boling, Vern Haynes, Thomas Jackson, Scott Harrell, William Hahn, Jerry Trotter, Herb Howard, John Reyna, Richard Crecelius, Ed Rowell, Dan Nelson, Chris Cowan, Brent Deffenbacher, Sam Burky, and Cliff Howery who shared their stories with us.

We are also grateful to Anita Harriger and Esther Greenwalt who proofread the drafts of the book.

PREFACE

S itting in a window seat, Roger Williams III was looking forward to thumbing through a magazine on a short flight from Sacramento to attend a National Youth Ministry Conference in San Diego, California. He'd fastened his seat belt, made sure his chair was in the full upright position, his tray table was locked and that his luggage was properly stowed when two well-dressed Ally McBeal look-a-likes sat down next to him.

Their conversation competed for attention with his magazine. They talked about the club scene–what they enjoyed drinking, whom they were "dating," their intimate relationships with men, both single and married. Then it turned into a gripe session.

"Why do guys have such a hard time committing?" One asked. "And why don't they ever leave their wives like they promise to?" Another complained.

They talked about work for a while, and about the time Williams was tuning out, one of them said, "But you know, if it wasn't for church, my life would really be hell." By now, Williams was only pretending to read his magazine, they had his full attention. "Wow, you go to church too. I know exactly how you feel. If it wasn't for church, I don't know where I'd be." "Yea, I know what you mean," the other lady said, "If I miss more than two weeks of church everything in my life goes nuts."

The plane started its descent into San Diego, everything got quiet, and Williams sat still--stunned by what he'd just heard. These women weren't genuine "seekers"-- people looking for the truth. Instead, they were going to church getting their religious fix.

After spending the first 20 years of his ministry as a Youth Pastor, Williams disembarked from the plane with a new determination. Today, he is in the middle of a new church plant "Start Church" in Stockton, California. "Our goal is not isolation from or accommodation to the culture," Williams said, "but a head-on interaction with the culture to see people transformed by the grace and mercy found in Jesus Christ."

These women on the plane didn't need a sermon on "Five steps to success." They didn't need a band-aid. They needed transformation. They were getting a faith-inoculation, when they needed an antidote for sin. They needed a church that would confront them, not accommodate them. They needed a church that would get past their felt needs and speak to their greatest need—to confess their sin and turn to Christ.

Some Christians criticize the lost, behind their back, but never proclaim the transforming power of the gospel to their face. Others, will try to help them get their lives cleaned up, but never ask them to change. Sinners don't need someone to make them feel bad or make them feel good. They need someone to tell them about Christ, who can transform their lives.

God is in the business of transforming lives. Paul wrote: "Therefore if any man be in Christ, he is a new creature: old things are passed away; behold, all things are become new." (2 Cor. 5:17 KJV)

And facilitating transformations is our business! "We are in the business to do ministry to facilitate transformation," Barna said at a Barna 2000/2001 Conference. "That is the only reason we exist."(San Jose, 11-06-2000)

Read along, and learn how you can facilitate someone's transformation. In the first section, "Transformed Lives," you'll encounter people whose lives were radically transformed by the power of God. Some instantly, others required a double touch. Still others relapsed after the conversion and others didn't come to Christ until they hit rock bottom. But they all have one thing in common, they are "new creatures in Christ."

In the second section, "Transformed Hearts" Tom Stringfellow shows what a transformed heart looks like. And in the third section, Randy McWhorter shows you how you can become a "Transformed Witness."

Section I: Transformed Lives
by Jim L. Wilson

Chapter 1
"Transformations"

The gun shot rang through the school yard. The bullet missed Pat and lodged in the doorpost. Pat ducked into the classroom as Reuben, scattered with the rest of the kids. Reuben found a place to stash the gun and went back into class. That night, he snuck out of his house, retrieved the gun and put it back in his family's gun case.

No one squealed and Reuben was never caught. But from that moment, something inside him wasn't the same.

Reuben was a good kid, he worked hard to make good grades in school. No wonder the school never suspected that it would be him that tried to kill Pat. Neither did it surprise the administrators that someone was trying to kill Pat, he was a known gang member and shootings, though not an every day occurrence at West Mesa High, weren't unusual either.

The next time Reuben saw Pat, he told him, "Next time I won't miss, you and your gang members better back off."

Pat's gang had been trying to recruit Reuben to join with them the whole school year. When Reuben wouldn't go along with them, they began harassing him. Finally, he had enough and packed a gun with him to school.

One of the Security Guards noticed the pressure Reuben was under and guessed that it was him that fired the shot. He knew Reuben was a good kid that just needed a break so he told him he could use his address to get into a better school district where he could get away from the gang activities. Reuben transferred and a few years later, he graduated.

When Greg invited Reuben to come to church with him, he didn't know anything about his background. They were coaching a little league team together and the invitation was natural.

Reuben didn't trust Greg. For one, he was white, and for another, he was on staff at the church, but Reuben's wife was interested in going to church. So they did.

And with time, Reuben's life was transformed by the power of the gospel. It's a good thing, because he was about to come face-to-face with the man he once tried to kill.

Reuben got a call to do some work at the Intel plant across town in Rio Rancho. As he was walking down the hall, he saw a face he hadn't seen in years–a face he could never forget–he saw Pat. Instead of the old hatred welling up inside him, Reuben felt conviction.

"Can I talk to you a minute?" Reuben asked. "A lot has happened since we were kids in High School, and I wanted to tell you that not long ago, I became a Christian and I wanted to ask you to forgive me for trying to kill you."

Choked up, Pat responded. "Me too. Three weeks after you shot at me, I made a decision to follow Christ."

Once enemies, now brothers.

In the weeks that followed, Reuben went to Pat's church to tell the story, and Pat went to Reuben's church–each testifying about the transforming power of the gospel. A gospel that changes lives.

HABLA ESPAÑOL?

Sitting alone in a neatly arranged circle of cold metal chairs was a bald-headed, extremely pregnant white girl with the word "SKIN" tattooed on the back of her hand and a pack of cigarettes under her chair. It had been years, but Jennifer had attended this church when she was a little girl. She was back because she remembered the love her teachers showed

7

her there, and increasingly, she doubted that she was doing the right thing with her life.

A man dressed in a blue, double-breasted blazer, red tie and tan pants, walked in the room, looked startled when he saw Jennifer, said "Hello" and darted back into the hallway.

In a minute, he returned, shared a moment of small talk, and then left the room again. Jennifer didn't say much that day, but she did listen.

The next Sunday she was back. This time more pregnant than the week before, wearing the same clothes and with her pack of cigarettes under the chair. But this week she shared her story. It turns out she just returned from Idaho where she was a part of a Neo-Nazi Camp with the mission of procreating the Aryan race. After getting pregnant with her second child, she fled the camp and was hiding from the skinheads but was searching for peace.

One evening, someone came up to the pastor and said, "There's someone out front smoking, will you go out there and tell her to stop?" Knowing exactly who it was, the pastor responded, "I'd rather have her here and smoke than not have her here at all."

With time, the power of God transformed Jennifer. She had the tattoo lasered off her hand, let her hair grow out and eventually married a wonderful man—a Hispanic man who didn't speak English. She learned his language.

Jennifer didn't need a change in behavior or learn to become more sociable skinhead, she needed a changed heart. Something God specializes in.

He did it for Jennifer, and He did it for "David" too.

FROM GAY TO JOYFUL

As a teenage boy, David noticed that he was more attracted to other boys than girls, but not wanting to give into those feelings, he did like the other boys did in his small southern town, he dated girls.

After graduating from college, he asked "Brenda" to marry him. But try as he might, he couldn't break from his obsession. After less than a year, he left Brenda, and moved to West Hollywood, California where he was free to act on his impulses. He never told Brenda why he left. He just left.

David lived the lifestyle. He went from one encounter to the next, until he settled down in a steady relationship and moved in with a man full time. Unlike some in the gay community, he was never careless in his sexual behavior. David always used "protection" and was regularly tested for HIV.

But the condom didn't protect his soul.

One evening, David's lover and several of his gay friends went to a nice restaurant to enjoy an evening out. Before long, David was observing himself interact with the people at the table. He literally got sick to his stomach.

The next Sunday, he went to church. The people welcomed him and he felt at home. He loved hearing the old hymns from his childhood. The next week he went back, and after a couple of months, made an appointment to speak to the pastor.

His upper lip trembled as he reached in his shirt pocket to pull out a list of things he needed to talk about. He told the pastor that he was gay and was openly living the homosexual lifestyle, open to everyone, that is, except his wife and family back home. "I've come to despise what I've become," David said, "And want to change, but what I want to know is, will these feelings I have toward men go away if I go back to my wife."

"No," the Pastor said. "In fact, they will intensify." David looked startled. as the Pastor continued. "Satan will entice you even more if you try to walk away from this lifestyle." It got quiet in the room.

The pastor continued, "The lifestyle you're living is unnatural—that's why AIDS is such a risk in the homosexual community. The body wasn't designed to do the things you've been doing with it." "I could give you a thousand examples to prove what you're saying," David said. "But not only is it unnatural," the pastor continued, "It is unbiblical. The scripture calls it an 'abomination.'"

David looked away. "Besides," the pastor said, "Do you think it is fair to ask your wife to take you back after you've betrayed her trust the way you have?" Instead of asking her to move out here and quit her job, you go back and tell her what you've become, beg her forgiveness, quit your job and move back to where she is and start dating her again."

They visited some more. After the hour for the appointment passed, David, folded up his list, thanked the pastor for his time and stood up to leave. "Before you go," the pastor said, "Let me answer a question you didn't ask—it will be worth it—it is the right thing to do."

They prayed together.

10

As David walked out the office door back to his car, the pastor thought to himself, *I'll never see him again.* He was wrong. The next Sunday he was back, and the next and the next.

About a month later, David made another appointment with the pastor to update him on what's happened. "I've moved out of my lover's house," David said, "and am working to reconcile things with my wife. I don't know if we'll get back together or not, but I feel so good about what I'm doing. There's another question I want to ask you," he said. "I'm not sure I'm saved, can you show me how to become a Christian?"

"Now that's an easier question," the pastor said with a chuckle. "I'd love to."

That day, David put his trust in Jesus. For a while, it looked like he and his wife would reconcile, but it never happened. Not yet at least. A couple of months later, David entered the baptismal waters with his pastor. Not the same old David—he was a new creation in Christ, transformed, by the power of the gospel.

Chapter 2
"In An Instant!"

Few people's lives illustrate the word "transformation" like Saul of Tarsus.

Before his encounter with Christ on the Road to Damascus, Saul was the poster child for Judaism. If they had elections for that sort of thing, Saul's peers would surely elect him as the "Most Valuable Member" at his Synagogue. They would do so because of his pedigree and his zeal.

Paul did not convert to Judaism, he was born into the faith. In fact, he was a member of the tribe of Benjamin, the aristocracy of the Race. Benjamin was the son of Jacob's old age from his favorite wife Rachel. He was Jacob's favorite son and his descendants lived their life with a special pride in their ancestry. Saul was as proud to be a Benjamite as an American would be proud to discover they descended from George Washington or Abraham Lincoln.

Saul had more reasons to be proud than his lineage, he was a righteous man. From a child, Saul was raised to be righteous. His parents circumcised him on the eighth day, just as the law prescribed, and unlike other Jews who became Hellenized under the reign of Rome, his family retained the distinction of speaking Hebrew, their mother tongue. They were "Hebrews of Hebrews."

As Saul matured, he became a Pharisee. Because of the conflicts Jesus had with the Pharisees, we often have a negative connotation about Pharisees. But to a Jew, there was not a higher goal to attain than to be a Pharisee. They were "separatists," adherents of the law who sought to live blameless lives before God. During Saul's time, they were about 6000 strong in Jerusalem, the largest and most influential religious party within Judaism.   Saul was blameless in matters of the law.   In other words, Saul wasn't just a "blue–blood," or a person with pedigree, he was living out his destiny, to be the best Jew he could be.

Not only was he living out his destiny, Saul was zealous to destroy those who would threaten the way of life he was born into, he devoted his life to destroying those who *perverted* Judaism with claims that the Messiah came, was crucified and rose from the dead.

One afternoon, Saul was traveling to Damascus to round up any people belonging to "the way," bind them and bring them back to Jerusalem where they would receive a "fair trial" before they were executed. On the road, he didn't meet anyone belonging to "the way," but he did meet someone who claimed to be "the way, the truth and the life"–he met the resurrected Lord.

A bright light–the bright and morning star–blinded him, and Saul dropped to the ground. Disoriented, Saul heard a voice from heaven asking why he was persecuting Him. (Acts 9:1-9)

Saul would never be the same. The blinding light, helped him to really see.   Saul left his life as a Pharisee and converted to "the way."   Before he died for his faith, he became a church planter, establishing the very churches he worked so hard to destroy.

His life was transformed. In an instant.

Sometimes, that's the way it works. God turns a person's life around instantaneously.   That's what happened with Craig.

LEROY BROWN

Actually, Craig's name could have been named Leroy Brown, because he was the *baddest* man in his whole town. Craig didn't just use drugs. He didn't just sell drugs, Craig was a drug enforcer–the guy that collects money from dealers who don't pay the supplier. He was one bad dude.

Craig lived on the outskirts of town with his wife and three children in a 24-foot travel trailer. When his children made a decision for Christ, Pastor Richard came out to his trailer to see if he could baptize them. Craig refused to come outside to talk to the preacher, so Richard asked if he could come inside.

Craig was wearing dirty blue jeans, had long greasy hair, tattoos all over his body and a permanent scowl on his face. *This has got to be the meanest man I've ever seen*, the pastor thought, *what am I doing here?* There was no place for the Pastor to sit. Craig sat in his chair and the preacher stood.

Pastor Richard worked up his courage and said, "Your children made a decision for Christ down at the church this week and we'd like to baptize them." Craig's answer was short, but not so sweet, "No, we're Catholic."

We'll, that's that, the Pastor thought as he left the trailer. But Richard didn't give up. Instead he developed a friendship with Craig.

A few weeks into the friendship, Richard shared the plan of salvation with Craig. Craig's answer was "no," but he did agree to let his kids be baptized.

Richard didn't stop trying.

It took some doing, but Richard convinced his buddy Craig to go to a Promise Keepers event with him in Stockton, CA. Under the conviction of the Holy Spirit, "bad, bad Leroy Brown" gave his life to Jesus. That was on a Friday, the next Sunday, Pastor Richard baptized him.

"Everybody knows what he was," Pastor Richard said, "and now nobody can believe what he's become." Today he's clean and sober, has a legitimate job and always has a big smile on his face. Everywhere he goes, he talks about Jesus.

His life was permanently transformed, by the same one who confronted Saul on the road to Damascus.

Just like He did with "Judy."

PROCLAIMING CHRIST IN LIFE AND DEATH

Judy slipped into the service late and took a back row seat in the small church on Hilton Head Island. Her cheeks were hollow, her skin was leathery and she had a distant look in her eyes–like nobody was home. Judy looked old for her age. Years of drug abuse robbed the twenty-six-year-old of her youth and vitality. She needed help, so she turned to the Lord. At first, she fidgeted in her seat, but soon, she sat still and listened.

When Christ saved her, He turned her life around. She didn't just forsake her past lifestyle, she began ministering to those she knew from her former life. The first person she led to the Lord was someone she introduced to drugs in her "other" life.

I wish, I could tell you that Judy is busy spreading the gospel today, but I can't. Eight months after her conversion, she died in a tragic accident. She shared her small bed room with her Saint Bernard dog. The dog, and her space heater used up all the available oxygen in the room and she died in her sleep.

Her death, tragic as it was, was not it vain. "At the funeral," her pastor said, "homosexuals and drug addicts attended. Her death opened the door for us to minister to her friends at the funeral and afterward."

The Apostle Paul wrote: For to me to live is Christ, and to die is gain. (Philip. 1:21 KJV) For the eight months Judy lived after her conversion, it was for Christ, and when she died, she gained an inheritance that was fit for a child of the king.

15

People who are transformed often use their former life as a platform to spread the transforming power of Jesus. Whether their life was filled with sin or just frustration, they find a way to help others like them, find the hope they know.

That's what Janet did.

THROUGH THE FOG

Try as she might, Janet couldn't focus. She tried to listen as Dan explained to her what it meant to be a Christ follower and how she could have a personal relationship with Jesus Christ, but she just couldn't get it.

But she didn't give up. She returned week after week to the "New Beginnings" class at her Church and listened as Dan patiently told her again how she could know Christ, but it just didn't register.

There was a fog she couldn't get through. And then there were the headaches and the fainting spells. What was happening?

The last thing she remembered was walking into the kitchen.

The doctors explained to her that her friend found her, unconscious on the floor and rushed her to the hospital. After extensive testing they believe she has a brain tumor that needs to be removed.

Janet signed the permission form and the doctors cut a hole in her head to remove the tumor. When she recovered, the fog was gone and she could concentrate again.

She returned to her church and enrolled in the "New Beginnings" class again. This time when Dan presented the gospel to her, everything clicked, and she placed her trust in Jesus.

Today she is a radical follower of Jesus Christ, ministering in Jesus' name to people with brain tumors. She organized the "hole in the head gang" as a support group where she can touch people who are hurting and present the gospel to them.

Sometimes, God uses the very thing that keeps us from enjoying life as a platform to touch hurting people, and when He does, our pain becomes His glory.

The transforming power of the resurrection can turn a persecutor of the church into a church planter, a drug enforcer into a spiritual man who prays with others, a person who gets people hooked on drugs into a person who gets people hooked on Jesus, and a person who can't understand the gospel into someone who explains it to people like her.

And sometimes that transformation takes place in an instant.

Chapter 3
"As A Process"

L
ike I mentioned in the previous chapter, the first thing I think of when I hear the word "transformation" is the sudden, radical change that happened in Saul of Tarsus' life when he met the Risen Lord on the Road to Damascus. Perhaps it is the stark contrast resulting from the encounter or maybe it is the relatively short time the change took that grabs my attention, I'm not sure. But one thing I'm sure of, even when the change happens instantaneously, there is a process involved.

We often don't notice the process and only focus on "the moment of change." It is all a matter of perspective. If you take a pencil and hold it in front of your face, with the eraser on the left and the lead to the right, you will see an object, about seven inches in length. But you can rotate the pencil 90 degrees until all you can see is the eraser. So, is the pencil a yellow object seven inches in length or is it a pink object, about a quarter of an inch in diameter? From one perspective, it appears as a pink object, a quarter of an inch in diameter, but when it is rotated to give a third dimension, it is easy to see that it is a yellow object about seven inches in length.

Is the perceptive that Salvation is only a point in time inadequate? Was Saul's salvation instantaneous? Well, yes. The encounter on the Road to Damascus was a defining moment. But before you miss the pencil for the eraser, consider the Lord's words to Ananias in Acts 9:15. "Go! This man is my chosen instrument to carry my name before the Gentiles and their kings and before the people of Israel." (NIV)

What time frame does the phrase "chosen instrument"

suggest? Did God's act of "choosing" and the blinding light happen at the same time? The Apostle Paul didn't view it that way. In Ephesians 1:4, he wrote, "According as he hath chosen us in him before the foundation of the world, that we should be holy and without blame before him in love." (NIV)

Before God created the world, He looked through eternity into time and chose Saul of Tarsus to become a witness to the Gentiles, and their kings and the people of Israel. There is a sense in which Saul's transformation began before he was even born. It began in the heart of God in eternity.

But another pertinent question is, did Saul's transformation end on the Road to Damascus? Or did it continue the rest of his life?

Saul followed the Lord's instructions and went to see Ananias and Ananias followed the Lord's instructions and met with Saul. Both actions were an exercise of faith. Saul blindly following the word of the Lord, literally. And Ananias following the word of the Lord with his eyes wide open.

I'm not sure which is harder.

Imagine how you would react if the Lord asked you to go and speak to someone who had a reputation for killing Christians? Would you be excited about that visitation assignment?

I'm not sure how excited he was, but Ananias was obedient.

"Then Ananias went to the house and entered it. Placing his hands on Saul, he said, 'Brother Saul, the Lord--Jesus, who appeared to you on the road as you were coming here--has sent me so that you may see again and be filled with the Holy Spirit.' [18] Immediately, something like scales fell from Saul's eyes, and he could see again. He got up and was baptized, [19] and after taking some food, he regained his strength. Saul spent several days with the disciples in Damascus." (Acts 9:17-19 NIV)

After meeting with Ananias, Saul was baptized. That act was an act of obedience, but it was also the way Saul entered into the church. And in doing so, he was submitting his soul to the care of the disciples, who spent several days with Saul, teaching him the ways of the Lord.

So in a sense, Saul was saved, Saul is saved, and Saul will be saved. Transformation has past, present and future ramifications.

THREE TENSES

Theologians often explain the three tenses of salvation with the words justified, sanctified and glorified. They use the word "justification" to explain "the point in time" someone is saved, "sanctification" as the process of growing in the Christian faith, and "glorification" to describe the future state of the believer as they enter into the presence of God in heaven.

Another way to put this process is to say that in "justification" we are freed from the penalty of sin, in "sanctification" we are freed from the power of sin and in "glorification" we are freed from the presence of sin.

These are helpful distinctions, and make for a neat theological package, but they do not fully explain the three tenses of transformation as the Apostle Paul saw them. Did you know that in the Book of Romans, Paul uses the word "justify" to refer to all three tenses of Salvation?

In Romans 8:30, justification is something that occurred in the past. He wrote, "Moreover whom he did predestinate, them he also called: and whom he called, them he also justified: and whom he justified, them he also glorified." (KJV) Also notice that glorification, a word we use theologically in the future tense is also in the past tense in this text.

Paul used justification in the present tense in Romans 5:1 when he wrote, "Therefore being justified by faith, we have peace with God through our Lord Jesus Christ." (KJV) and in Romans 3:24 when he wrote: " Being justified freely by his grace through the redemption that is in Christ Jesus." (KJV)

But Paul didn't limit justification to what happens in the past and present tense, he also saw it as something God does in the future. In Romans 3:30, Paul wrote, "Seeing it is one God, which shall justify the circumcision by faith, and uncircumcision through faith."

How can that be? How can transformation be rooted in the past, active in the present and secure in the future?

I like the way Frances Havergal, the rector at St Nicholas, in Worcester put it in his 19th Century hymn, "Like a River Glorious." He wrote, "Perfect, yet if floweth fuller every day; Perfect, yet it groweth deeper all the way."

I have a feeling the Apostle Paul would approve of Havergal's theology. At the "point in time" of our conversion, we are perfectly transformed, yet every day our faith and our transformation is fuller and grows deeper.

Like every relationship, our relationship with the Lord grows as we walk with him. And we become more like he wants us to be.

Not only are transformations processes, some of them are slow, tedious and gradual. Sometimes they are so slow, the contrast is camouflaged by the repetitive tick of the clock. Have you ever seen time-lapsed photography of a seed's germination process? With the clock sped up, the roots extend, the small shoot emerges and a plant begins to grow. But who would have the patience to watch the process without the benefit of time lapse photography? The change is so gradual it will go unnoticed to the naked eye.

Patience is not only a virtue, it is also a rare commodity. I stand at a microwave, for sixty seconds to heat up my coffee and complain that it is taking too long. Fast food can never be served fast enough to suit me, and the Information Super Highway often feels gridlocked to me when it takes more than

10 seconds for a web page to load.

PERSISTENT PRAYER

But sometimes, transformations take time, like it did for Joe Arnott. For sixty years the members of Oak Grove Baptist Church in Mount Carmel, Tennessee prayed for Joe Arnott to come to Christ. Even though he wasn't a Christian, he was a religious man and attended Sunday School and Church for all those years, but never accepted Christ as his Savior and Lord.

Several church members witnessed to him, but his answer was always the same, "I'm not ready yet." No one gave up, they kept praying for him.

March 5, 2000 their prayers were answered. Arnott made a public profession of his faith. The congregation wept as they watched 60 years of prayers walk the isle to give his life to Jesus. Seeing what was happening, the men in his Sunday School class followed Arnott down the isle and stood with him as he made his decision.

His pastor, Benny Keck said, "I suppose fewer words will ever sound sweeter to my ears than hearing Joe say, 'I believe that Jesus is the Christ, the Son of the Living God.'" (BP, 5-12-2000)

Sixty years? Sound unusual? That's how long it took for Roy too.

FROM LEGALISM TO LIFE

Roy regularly attended church as a child, but was raised in a bazaar, legalistic church family. At church, his dad was a pillar, active in the church and even served as a deacon, but at home he was an abusive monster.

As soon as he could, Roy bolted from the church and wanted nothing to do with it. He was a crude, rude man who looked out for number one. He didn't pretend to be one thing at church, while he was something else at home, he didn't pretend at all. Roy was a scoundrel and a cheat, and he didn't care who knew it.

When he turned 60, Roy started coming to church again. He'd walk in late, sit on the back row and listen for a while, but would always leave before the service ended. Bro. Scott would try to witness to Roy, but he wouldn't have anything to do with the gospel or those hypocrites down at the church.

But he kept coming to church. Listening and watching, but mostly watching the people. Within a couple of years, God got a hold of him, and changed Roy's life. "The people loved him to Christ." Bro. Scott said, "today he is a sweet loving man."

Roy's transformation took sixty years. It doesn't always happen in an instant, sometimes it takes time.

PERSISTENT WITNESS

For Frank, it didn't take sixty years, but it took a long time. Frank must have thought, *what part of "no" doesn't this guy understand? Every time I see him, he keeps trying to shove religion down my throat. When is he going to stop?* After a while, Frank became so enraged by John's constant witness that he'd curse at John when he'd share his faith.

For John, it wasn't personal with Frank, he loved the Lord and talked about Him with his truck driving buddies at breaks and stops. John wasn't trying to force anybody to do anything, he was just excited about his faith so he talked about it.

Sometimes, John would only talk to a person once and they'd make a decision to follow Christ. That's the way it was with the guy he met while picking up canned apple sauce in Yakima, Washington. John was waiting to be loaded when he saw the big guy out of the corner of his eye. The guy was 6' 5" if he was an inch.

John walked over, and began talking about his family, before you know it, he was talking about his Lord and the big guy was choking up and starting crying. That day, beside a loading dock in Yakima, Washington, the man found Christ. John never saw him again.

That's not the way it was with Frank. They drove for the same company and saw each other several times a week. And every time they saw each other, the conversation would turn to matters of faith.

Frank never listened, that is until his family began to fall apart. That time he sought John out, and after hearing the gospel again, he placed his faith in Christ. Today, Frank is still having conversations with truck drivers about Christ, but this time, it is him doing the talking. Frank's life was forever transformed, over a period of time.

Chapter 4
"The Double Touch"

The great hymn writer, John Newton wrote, "Amazing grace! How sweet the sound, That saved a wretch like me! I once was lost, but now am found, Was blind but now I see." What a powerful metaphor to describe transformations–going from being blind to being able to see!

But Saul of Tarsus and some other people in the New Testament, it wasn't a metaphor, it is their testimony. Saul's transformation from a persecutor of the church to a church planter. On the road to Damascus, he encountered a bright light that blinded him. Following the instructions the Lord gave him, he went to meet with Ananias who healed his blindness and coached him in his new faith. Other people regained their sight by Jesus' touch.

Some of the transformations, like Saul of Tarsus' were immediate. That's the way it was for Bartimaeus, a blind beggar who sat by the road to Jericho. One day, as he sat begging by the roadside, he heard a crowd walking by. When he asked someone why there was such a big crowd, they told him Jesus was walking by. "And when he heard that it was Jesus the Nazarene, he began to cry out and say, 'Jesus, Son of David, have mercy on me!'" (Mark 10:47)

The crowd didn't like the commotion Bartimaeus was causing, so they rebuked him and told him to quiet down. But Bartimaeus kept begging for mercy, and Jesus called for him. "And casting aside his cloak, he jumped up, and came to Jesus. [51] And answering him, Jesus said, 'What do you want Me to do for you?' And the blind man said to Him, 'Rabboni, I want to regain my sight!' [52] And Jesus said to him, 'Go your way; your faith has made you well.' And

25

immediately he regained his sight and began following Him on the road." (Mark 10:46-52)

All Jesus had to do was speak and the man was healed. Notice that the transformation was immediate. Just like it was with a pair of blind men that Jesus healed. Once again, Jesus was walking when someone cried out for mercy. Jesus went into the house and the blind men pursued him. When Jesus saw them, He asked, . "'Do you believe that I am able to do this?' They said to Him, 'Yes, Lord.' [29] Then He touched their eyes, saying, 'Be it done to you according to your faith.' [30] And their eyes were opened." (Matthew 9:29-30)

This time, instead of simply speaking to the men, Jesus touched their eyes and when he did, their eyes were immediately opened.

Another time, Jesus was walking past a blind man, who was blind from birth. The disciples asked Jesus why the man was blind, was it because of his sin or a sin of his parents. "Jesus answered, 'It was neither that this man sinned, nor his parents; but it was in order that the works of God might be displayed in him.'" (John 9:3)

Without the man saying anything, Jesus spat on the ground and applied the mud on the man's eyes, and told the man to go and wash his eyes in the pool of Siloam. I'm not sure how hard it was to access the pool in Jesus' time, but today, it is eighteen feet below the surrounding ground and can only be reached by walking down a steep flight of stone steps. (ZPEB, v5, p. 437)

Why would Jesus send a blind man on a precarious errand like this? Couldn't He just pronounce him healed like he did Bartimaeus or touch his eyes like he did the two blind men? I don't know for certain, but perhaps it had something to do with the conversation He'd just had with His disciples.

Don't you imagine the blind man was humiliated by what the disciples asked Jesus? I mean, he was blind, but he

26

wasn't deaf. He heard every word. When Jesus sent this man on the errand, he restored his dignity. He wasn't helpless, he was a healthy man with a disability–certainly he could navigate a few steps to wash his face.

When he returned, he could see. Another immediate transformation.

On one occasion Jesus spoke to a man and he regained his sight, another time He touched two men and they were healed, and another time, he put mud on a man's eyes and asked him to wash the mud away in a pool before he would see. Each time, the circumstances and the point of contact were different, but each time the healing was immediate. But there was a time in scripture where a blind man wasn't fully healed until he received a double touch.

"And they came to Bethsaida. And they brought a blind man to Him, and entreated Him to touch him. [23] And taking the blind man by the hand, He brought him out of the village; and after spitting on his eyes, and laying His hands upon him, He asked him, 'Do you see anything?' [24] And he looked up and said, 'I see men, for I am seeing them like trees, walking about.' [25] Then again He laid His hands upon his eyes; and he looked intently and was restored, and began to see everything clearly" (Mark 8:22-25)

Why did Jesus have to touch this man twice for him to be able to see? I don't have a clue. Certainly Jesus has the power to heal the blind instantaneously. But this time, it took a double touch. I can't explain why, but I do know that's the way it works sometimes. That's certainly the way it worked with Ray.

A PHYSICAL AND A SPIRITUAL BIRTH

Pastor Tom couldn't help notice Ray's family as they walked in the church. For one thing, this was Tom's first church and it was small enough that he noticed any new people who walked into the auditorium, but this family caught

27

his eye quickly.

Three things caught his attention. One was the stale smell of cigarette smoke that followed them in the room, another was Ray's wife, she was pregnant, uncomfortably pregnant–it looked like she was ready to have that baby at any moment. And the third thing he noticed was the older woman who walked in next to the couple's young daughter.

Auntie Vivian was her name. "When Ray called to ask if I'd come out to help out with the new baby and all," Aunt Vivian said, "I said, I'd only come on one condition: that we find a church in the area and attend together."

Ray hadn't been to church in ten years, not since he was a child, but he knew he needed help when the new baby was born, so he agreed to the conditions Aunt Vivian set out.

It was obvious to Tom that Ray didn't want to be there, and when he heard Aunt Vivian's story, he understood why. But he was glad they were there, regardless of the reason why.

That morning, Tom preached a simple Gospel message to the small crowd that gathered and when he extended the invitation, Ray's entire family walked forward to accept Christ.

The small girl seemed sincere in her desire to know Christ and Ray's wife was in tears, but the look on Ray's face communicated that he was willing to go along with the family's decision, but Tom wasn't sure if Ray was thrilled about it.

Is it just a part of pleasing Aunt Vivian, Tom thought, *or is Ray sincere?*

Later in the week, Tom called to see if he could schedule a followup visit with the family. Aunt Vivian answered the phone and told him that if he wanted to see Ray, he'd have to go to the hospital, they were having their baby.   That's exactly what Tom did. But the baby arrived six hours before Tom did. After celebrating the new birth with the parents, Tom went over the plan of salvation with the couple again and talked to them about baptism. After visiting with them further, Tom was satisfied that they both were making a genuine decision for Christ.

As he was leaving the room, Ray said to him, "Pastor didn't you forget something?" "What do you mean?" Tom asked. "Aren't you going to talk to us about tithing?" Ray replied.

It had been years since Ray had been in church, but he did remember the sermons he'd heard about tithing. And he knew that if he was going to follow Christ, he was going to do it all the way. Ray reached into his pocket and pulled a pew envelope that he'd taken from the church the Sunday before. "Here's my tithe for this week." Ray said. "I didn't want to wait until next Sunday to give it."

A couple of weeks later, Ray invited Tom out to lunch with him. Ray took Tom to his favorite bar. "I know this isn't the kind of place you usually go to lunch," Ray said. "But I spent over $10,000.00 a month here entertaining my business associates over the last year, and I wanted to stop by to tell the owner why I wouldn't be in anymore, and I wanted you to be with me when I did."

Thirty years have passed since that day. Tom has gone on to pastor other churches and Ray has moved out of state. A lot of things have changed over those thirty years, but not one thing–Ray is still a radical follower of Jesus Christ.

It took a double touch. Once when he was a child, and once when he was an adult, but Christ transformed Ray's life.

Ray's moment of Salvation didn't come for him until adulthood, but it is impossible to overestimate the impact the first touch had on Ray's life. Isaiah 55:11 clearly teaches that God's word will not return unto Him void, but it will accomplish what God sends it out to accomplish. Sometimes the transformation is immediate, only requiring one touch, but sometimes the seed that is planted with one touch is harvest with another.

Paul wrote, "So then faith cometh by hearing, and hearing by the word of God." (Romans 10:17 KJV) Exposure to God's word is a spiritual catalyst. At least it was for Steve and Gail.

OCCUPYING A CHURCH PEW

Steve had a catholic background and really didn't want to go to the Baptist Church with his new bride, but it was the family's church and he felt obligated to keep the family's Sunday tradition. He tolerated their religious talk, but enjoyed the Sunday dinners at the in-laws.

Week after week, he sat on the pew and listened to the preacher talk. He didn't know it, but when he did, his in-laws were praying for his salvation. One week it happened, the gospel broke through his obligation and changed his heart. Today he isn't just sitting on that pew, he is active in the church's evangelism ministry, bringing other people to Christ.

NOT ME

"Gail" didn't think the gospel applied to her. Because of her Scientology background she didn't believe in hell, and since she didn't believe in hell, she didn't feel a personal need for salvation. But she did enjoy attending the prayer meeting for Spiritual Awakening held every Tuesday night at Grace Church. She enjoyed the people, the atmosphere, and oddly enough she enjoyed listening to the passionate prayers of the Christ followers that gathered for the meeting.

Whenever Pastor Cliff would present the gospel to her, she'd remind him that she didn't believe in hell and didn't need Salvation from anything, but she didn't seem the least bit offended by his persistence. She kept coming back.

Before long, Cliff began praying out loud for Gail's salvation at the meetings. Not only did he long for a spiritual awakening in the nation, he wanted one in his friend's heart.

One Monday, Gail stopped by Cliff's office to talk.

Patiently, Cliff listened for close to an hour as she spilled her problems. Finally, Cliff asked, "How miserable are you going to have to get before you give your heart to Christ?" "I don't know," she said. "Are you ready to take that 18 inch journey from your heart to your head and accept Christ as your Savior now?" Gail said yes, and Pastor Cliff prayed with her to receive Christ.

The next Tuesday night, Gail couldn't wait to come to the prayer meeting. When she did, she told the group that their prayers were answered for her salvation, then she joined them as they prayed for the spiritual awakening that happened in heart to happen across the nation.

Chapter 5
"After Relapse"

*W*ho could that be at this hour? William thought as he slipped on his house shoes. William flipped on the light in the living room and walked to the front door. With his hand on the deadbolt, he looked through the peep hole. When he recognized the man outside, he turned the deadbolt counterclockwise, and opened the door.

"Well hello, 'John.'" William said. "Come in." "Thanks, Preacher," John said, "Sorry to come by so late, but I didn't know where else to turn.

John's wife, "Mabel" was an active member at William's church, but not John. John was an alcoholic that would go on drinking binges for several months at a time. Mabel was always requesting prayer for John's salvation, and the church was faithful to pray for him whenever they gathered.

William could smell liquor on John's breath–he'd been drinking again, but this time, something was different. John talked a while and sobbed a while. He had hit the bottom, and was ready to turn to the Lord for help.

William listened. And when the time was right, he shared the plan of salvation with John. That night, John placed his trust in Jesus.

I wish I could tell you he never drank again, but I can't. "After I made that decision, I went out with the old buddies again." John said. "But it never left me, I knew I had to get back to God and be baptized."

With time, that's exactly what he did. He relapsed back into his old lifestyle after his Salvation, but finally, with the help of the Lord and the support of his church, he got it right. And when he did, John was able to defeat a sinful habit and became a vital part of the church that didn't give up on him.

Sometimes, God's transforming power changes people's lives in an instant, and the people never revert to their previous sinfulness, but sometimes, people's lives aren't transformed until after they've relapsed back into a lifestyle of sin.

SLIPPING AWAY

After Sam finished his first tour of duty as a Navy Seal in Viet Nam, his next billet was stateside pulling shore duty in the San Diego area. That's where he met Mark.

Mark was going through SEAL team training at the time, and would eventually end up on the same team with Sam, but they didn't meet at work, they met at church. Because Mark was training to become a SEAL and was a new believer, Sam took a special interest in him and they became friends.

Mark made it through the program and became a BUDS (Basic Underwater Demolition SEAL) instructor. He was making a success of himself, that is, until alcohol got the best of him. When his problem became disruptive at work, the Navy put him in rehabilitation, but it didn't take. His problem got so bad, that he lost his career and had to get out of the Navy. But his career isn't all he lost, he lost his family too. After a while, his wife had enough and she left him.

Mark had lost it all, except his salvation and his friendship with Sam. Even when the Navy and his wife didn't want Mark anymore, God still did. Romans 8:38-39 says, "For I am convinced that neither death nor life, neither angels nor demons, neither the present nor the future, nor any powers, [39] neither height nor depth, nor anything else in all creation, will be able to separate us from the love of God that is in Christ Jesus our Lord."

What can separate us from God's love? Notice the extremes Paul mentions when he answered that question. Death–life. Angels–demons. Present–future. Height–depth.

Nothing, absolutely, nothing can separate us from God's love.

I suppose that if it was Mark's responsibility to hold on to God, he would have slipped away years before, but it wasn't Mark that had to hold onto God, it was God that held onto Mark. Jesus said, "I give them eternal life, and they shall never perish; no one can snatch them out of my hand." (John 10:28 NIV)

What kind of life did Jesus promise in John 10:28? Eternal life, the scripture says. Life that doesn't end. Not life for as long as you walk a straight line–there is no condition to the promise–it is eternal.

"My Father, who has given them to me, is greater than all; no one can snatch them out of my Father's hand." (John 10:29 NIV)

God held Mark in the palm of his hand, even when Mark was drifting away from his commitment, God held him tightly. And Mark was certainly drifting.

For the next two years, Mark would stop by to chat with Sam but was continuing to live out of God's will. Sam patiently encouraged Mark to return to the Lord, but Mark would always say something to the effect of, "If God will do this or that, then I'll follow Him again."

One afternoon, Sam got fed up with Mark's rationalizations. He sprung out of his chair, grabbed Mark and threw him up against the wall. "When are you going to get your act together?" Sam yelled. "Get out of here, and don't come back until we have something new to talk about."

When Mark left, Sam prayed, "God, this guy doesn't deserve to breathe your air. Why don't you do us all a favor and just beam him up?"

Mark had grievously sinned against God and his sin was destroying every relationship he had. He'd lost his career, his wife, and now, he was losing his friend.

That's the way it is. Even if we don't lose our salvation when we live in habitual sin, we still lose a lot.

34

LOVING DISCIPLINE

King David, a man after God's own heart, grievously sinned against his God when he committed adultery with Bathsheba and had her husband killed to cover up his sin. Throughout the entire ordeal, God continued to love David, and when David's life was over, God showed David's descendants favor, because of David's heart. In 1 Kings 15:4-5 the scripture says, "Nevertheless, for David's sake the Lord his God gave him a lamp in Jerusalem by raising up a son to succeed him and by making Jerusalem strong. [5] For David had done what was right in the eyes of the Lord and had not failed to keep any of the Lord's commands all the days of his life--except in the case of Uriah the Hittite."

But don't think David wasn't disciplined for his sin. Rev. 3:19 says, "Those whom I love I rebuke and discipline. So be earnest, and repent." David was rebuked and disciplined.

The child born of his adultery died. One of his sons raped one of his daughters and another son rose up in rebellion against him and tried to overthrow his kingdom. David suffered greatly because of his sin.

But in the end, David was restored because he received the discipline and repented from his sin. Solomon wrote, "My son, do not despise the Lord's discipline and do not resent his rebuke," (Proverbs 3:11 NIV)

Receiving discipline isn't easy, but it is necessary.

Pastor Haynes met Willy at a gas station early one morning. The pastor was trying to sell a car and Willy was trying to sell some dope. Neither of them were buying that day, but Pastor Haynes did convince Willy to agree to come to church. After a while, Willy gave his life to Jesus, but he kept falling back into his old ways of selling dope and chasing women.

Every time he backslided, Pastor Haynes would dismiss him from his church positions, and tell him he had to get his life right before he could serve in the church again. The discipline didn't drive Willy out of the church, he'd say, "Don't give up on me Preacher, I'm going to get it right some day . . . I'll get it right."

Today, Willy is faithfully serving the Lord–he finally got it right. Love motivated the pastor to discipline Willy. He didn't discipline him in anger, it was in love.

God's love compelled Him to discipline David. And it made him a better person.

SELF INFLICTED PAIN

But sometimes the pain we feel from our sin isn't at God's hand, it is a natural consequence for our actions.

Mark couldn't blame God or the Navy for losing his career. The Navy isn't going to let a drunk be a BUDS instructor. Neither could Mark blame God that he lost his family. His wife deserved better, and she moved on. It wasn't God's fault. Mark designed his own nightmare.

When Sam finished his prayer, asking God to beam Mark up, he fell under conviction of the Holy Spirit for losing his patience with his friend. He began meditating on the transforming power of the resurrection, visualizing Jesus raising from the dead. And when he thought about Jesus coming out of the grave, he realized that for a time, he wore grave clothes.

That was Mark. He had experienced the power of the resurrection, but he never took off the old grave clothes.

Sam prayed again, "God, I'm sorry, I still think Mark is a sorry individual, but I know your transforming power and I know you can transform him." From then on, every time Mark came to Sam's mind, he prayed for him to take off the grave clothes and live in Christ's transforming power.

About a year later, Mark came by to see Sam again, but nothing had changed. He said the same old stuff, "If God will just . . .then I will . . ." This time, Sam didn't throw him against the wall, instead he looked him square in the eye and said, "Mark, God is God and He will only accept an unconditional surrender from you." And then Sam asked Mark: "Are you willing to surrender your life to Him now?"

Romans 13:12 b says, "So let us put aside the deeds of darkness and put on the armor of light." When Jesus raised Lazarus from the dead, he said, "'Lazarus, come out!' [44] The dead man came out, his hands and feet wrapped with strips of linen, and a cloth around his face. Jesus said to them, 'Take off the grave clothes and let him go.'" (John 11:43-44 NIV) Grave clothes are for the dead, not the living. Lazarus needed to take them off, and so did Mark.

Mark said, "yes." And he did. He took off the grave clothes, and began walking in the transforming power of the resurrection.

Today, Mark has remarried and is actively serving the Lord. His life radically transformed, by the power of God. And he is living his life wrapped in the armor of light, without grave clothes!

Chapter 6
"After 'Hitting The Bottom'"

Actions, the saying goes, "speak louder than words." Ungodly actions can muffle the sounds of righteous words. That's what happened in Stephanie's home.

SHOW ME, DON'T TELL ME

Stephanie grew up in church and regularly heard the claims of the gospel, but never experienced a life transformation until she was eighteen. She didn't just need to hear the gospel, she needed to see it. She couldn't see it, at least not at home. During the week, her Mom went from one man's bed to another, but on Sunday she would get dressed up and sit in church, pretending to be something she wasn't.

It's good that Stephanie's Mom attended church–that's where she needed to be. Sinners need to hear the gospel. But I don't think that was Stephanie's point of view.

Unfortunately, Stephanie made a choice to emulate the Mom she saw at home–the real Mom–not the Mom she saw at church. Stephanie's promiscuity wasn't her only problem, she became rebellious and starting running away from home and spent most of her teenage years in and out of trouble.

When she reached the bottom, she turned to Christ. "All these things [the gospel] I heard, but never quite experienced them until I was desperate and cried out." Stephanie said. "When I did, He was there."

After Stephanie "cried out to God," her life was transformed. Her spirit of rebellion was gone, and so was her foul mouth. Her attitude changed too. She went from roughness to sweetness overnight. Today she is twenty-six and is still walking by faith and serving the Lord. In her desperation, she found hope–she found God.

CRIME AND PUNISHMENT

Before he found Christ, "Bubba" hit bottom too.

Larry worked long, hard hours as the manager of a feedlot, but tried to find time to grow in his personal relationship with the Lord. After taking a four-week witnessing class at his church, he began to take a personal interest in one of his employees.

One afternoon he came straight from work to meet with Ed, his pastor. "Pastor," he said, "you need to go over to see Bubba today. "Why's that?" Pastor Ed asked. "He's in some big trouble; the police stopped by the feedlot today and said they would arrest him tomorrow. Pastor, you've got to go see him, he really needs the Lord." "I'll be glad to go with you to back you up," Pastor Ed said, "but you will need to do the talking." Reluctantly, Larry agreed.

Pastor Ed hopped in Larry's pickup and off they went. It was a long drive to Bubba's trailer–about 20 miles from the church-- the last five miles were a terrible dirt road. When they arrived, Pastor Ed was shocked at the living conditions. One corner of the trailer was sagging. There were old washing machines, junk cars and debris scattered all over the yard.

Reluctantly, Bubba invited them in. Old, broken-down furniture flanked the walls, a single 40-watt light bulb hung from the ceiling. Pastor Ed and Larry tried to cope with the foul smell as they sank into the couch.

It was an uncomfortable situation. Obviously, Bubba was embarrassed for his boss to see how he lived. Larry had a hard time getting to the point. The air was thick. Instead of rescuing Larry, Pastor Ed sat patiently as the evening unfolded. Finally, Bubba asked, "Well Larry, why did you come out here for?"

That was all the prompting Larry needed. "Bubba," Larry said, "your life's a mess and you need the Lord!" *Not exactly the approach I taught in class,* Pastor Ed thought. After a pause, Bubba said, "you're right–I do." Bubba prayed to receive Christ that night.

The prayer Bubba prayed didn't solve all his problems, the next day, the police came to the feedlot and took him away in handcuffs. But it did settle one thing–his eternal destiny.

LIFE IN A BOTTLE

Just like Bubba, Gary didn't find Christ until he had no place else to turn.

From across the street everything looked fine over at Gary's house. Really, he appeared to live an idyllic life, you might even say he was living "the good life." Gary rose to the top of his profession rather quickly, and his marriage seemed solid. After all, not everyone makes it past their tenth anniversary.

Gary was focused. In just three years at a Fortune 500 company, he had proven himself with hard work and dedication. His hard work was paying off, but it was also taking its toll on him.

Just to unwind after a hard day's work, Gary would enjoy a cold one. Often, on business trips, Gary would relax with Jack Daniels. Soon he was spending more time in the bottle than with his wife.

Until one day when his wife said, she'd had enough. Maybe it was because he spent so much time in the bottle, but Gary never saw the "other man" or the divorce coming.

The pain was more than he could bear, so he tried to drown it in his bottle.

Emilio, Gary's next door neighbor had prayed for months for the right time to share his faith with Gary. One afternoon, Gary crossed his driveway to talk to Emilio. At first, Emilio listened, but after a while, he shared the hope he'd found in Jesus with his hurting friend.

And with time, Gary placed his trust in Jesus. Gary's life isn't perfect now, he still has the residue from his past mistakes in his life, but now he has two friends to help him as he navigates life's challenges. One lives across the street. The other lives in his heart. (On Mission, July-Aug 2001, p. 29)

JOY RIDE

Charles was one of the lucky ones. He had fine Christian parents who saw that he attended church with them regularly. But when he turned eighteen, his luck ran out. He was hanging out with a couple of younger buddies when he stole a car to take it on a joy ride. Because they were minors, his friends got off easy, but not Charles–the prosecution tried him as an adult and he got jail time. Because it was his first offense, he only got a couple of months, but it was still jail time.

Sitting behind bars, the only thing Charles had was time. He had plenty of it, to sit and to think. As he sat on his bunk staring at the cinder block walls, he thought about what he did, his future, and he thought about the things he learned in Church. He knew he had a decision to make.

"When I had no place to turn," Charles said. "I turned to God."

Sometimes, that's how it happens. People grow up hearing the truth, but don't apply it to their life, for whatever reason, until they don't have any other options. Then they turn to God.

That's what happened to Jonah. From the belly of the fish, he prayed, "In my distress I called to the Lord, and he answered me. From the depths of the grave I called for help, and you listened to my cry. [3] You hurled me into the deep, into the very heart of the seas, and the currents swirled about

41

me; all your waves and breakers swept over me. [4] I said, 'I have been banished from your sight; yet I will look again toward your holy temple.' [5] The engulfing waters threatened me, the deep surrounded me; seaweed was wrapped around my head. [6] To the roots of the mountains I sank down; the earth beneath barred me in forever. But you brought my life up from the pit, O Lord my God. [7] When my life was ebbing away, I remembered you, Lord, and my prayer rose to you, to your holy temple." (Jonah 2:2-7 NIV)

Jonah's prayer was a prayer of desperation that a person groans when they are at the bottom. Verse 6 says he descended to the roots of the mountains, which to the ancients would mean at the bottom of the sea. From that deep, dark pit, he cried.

The Psalmist wrote, "He lifted me out of the slimy pit, out of the mud and mire; he set my feet on a rock and gave me a firm place to stand." (Psalm 40:2)

THE PIG PEN

For the psalmist the phrase "slimy pit" was a metaphor to express what it is like to be bogged down by sin and worry. But for the prodigal son, it wasn't a metaphor, it was his home.

When I was a teenager, my brother, my dad and I ran a few hogs and I spent more time than I'd like to admit in the pig pen. Today, I can't think of a worse place to be than a pig pen. The smell is bad, but after a while, you get used to it. What I never got used to was rainy season.

When it rained, the automatic feeder would get clogged and we'd have to unclog it so the animals could eat. As you know, pigs have sharp, narrow hooves that sink in mud. After a while, they will turn the hard ground into a slimy pit. After a really good rain, we'd sink down to our calves as we walked through the pen to get to the feeders.

Even with rubber boots on, that was disgusting, but then

there was the time I slipped and fell, face first into the slime. I looked up at Dad and said, "Well at least now I know how the Prodigal Son felt."

But really, I didn't. I may have known what it felt like to be knee-deep, face down in a "slimy pit." But I didn't know what it was like to a Jew, knee-deep, face down in a "slimy pit."

He had sunk as low as he could. To the Jews, swine were unclean animals and they weren't supposed to have anything to do with them.

Not only was the prodigal out of the will of his father, flat broke in a foreign land, but he was alone, in a pig pen, fighting with the pigs for something to eat. It seemed like a lifetime ago when he told his father to give him his inheritance so he could go out and live it up. Now, more than anything else, all he wanted to do was to go home.

At the bottom, he had no place to look, but up. I don't know why some people wait to reach bottom to look up. Maybe they think the rules don't apply to them and the world owes them something, or maybe they don't really see their need until they are completely needy.

COUNTY LOCKUP

Eric was a popular guy in High School. He was funny, charming and a star athlete, in fact, he was a state champion wrestler. Eric only had one problem–he was ugly. But that didn't keep him from being a "player." The girls all seemed to fall for his charm and before long, he'd use them, dispose of them, and move onto the next conquest.

At the prodding of his father, Todd, Eric's friend, asked him to come to church with him. Todd was surprised by Eric's response, he was happy to come.

The first thing Eric noticed was that there were some good looking girls in the youth group–it was, in his opinion, "a target rich environment." Naturally, he wanted to come back.

And he did. His primary motive was to hit on the girls, but while he was there, he did hear the gospel. He finally zeroed in on who he would ask out and was surprised when she turned him down. "I know the kind of boy you are," she said to him, "and I'm not interested in going out with you."

Eric didn't know how to take rejection. Not wanting to make "no" his final answer, he attended church for another year or two, but never got a date with the girl that turned him down.

One afternoon, Todd got a call from Eric. He was in trouble. "I have no one else to call." Eric said, "I got caught drinking and driving and I need some help."

At the county lockup, Todd looked at Eric through a plexiglass window and talked to him through a tinny speaker. For the first time in his life, Todd shared the gospel with someone and that day, Eric accepted Christ. Eric said, "I'd heard about Jesus being a Savior, but until I was in jail, there was nothing that I needed saving from. That's when I realized I needed a Savior."

It took being in jail for Eric to see his need, and it took living in the pig pen for the Prodigal Son to realize he needed a relationship with his father. Here's what the bible says

44

happened: "When he came to his senses, he said, 'How many of my father's hired men have food to spare, and here I am starving to death! [18] I will set out and go back to my father and say to him: Father, I have sinned against heaven and against you. [19] I am no longer worthy to be called your son; make me like one of your hired men.'" (Luke 15:17-19 NIV)

GOING HOME

Finally, after hitting rock bottom, the son, "came to his senses." He did just as he said he would. He got up out of the "slimy pit" and took the first step toward home. One step followed another until he could see the old homestead.

But before he could see his father, his father saw him and began to run to him. The dad threw his arms around the son and kissed him. The boy began his speech–"I have sinned against heaven and in your sight; I am no longer worthy to be called your son." But before he could finish, the father interrupted and called for his servants. Look at my son, he doesn't have proper clothes. Get him a robe, and some sandals, and put a family ring on his finger! My dead son is now alive, let's celebrate! (Luke 15:20-24 personal paraphrase)

Eric's jail house conversion was as genuine as the Prodigal Son's pig pen conversion. It changed his life forever. He got clean and sober and sought counseling for his problem of being a sexual predator. He enrolled in Bible College and started working with the Fellowship of Christian Athletes.

Today he is a Christian counselor, helping sexual predators turn their lives around. Eric is no longer a player, he is a devoted family man. Loving his adopted daughter and her mother–his wife. His life forever transformed, by the power of God.

Oh, did I mention that the woman he married was a rape victim? Once traumatized by a sexual predator, she now is safe and secure in the arms of a man who without Christ was like the man that raped her, but now, because of the transforming power of God, Eric is her knight in shining armor.

Section II: Transformed Hearts
by Tom Stringfellow

On September 11, 2001 American patriotism was reborn. Within minutes of the collapse of the World Trade Center twin towers, American heroes emerged–fire fighters, medical personnel, and policemen, many of whom lost their lives, construction workers, cab drivers, and sanitation workers. Service men and women lost their lives while in offices instead of on ships or in fighter jets. People from all professions and walks of life were transformed, in the blink of an eye, from ordinary citizens to citizen heroes.

Within hours many more joined the ranks of the heroic. Mayors, governors, and other civic officials addressed the needs for recovery from such a tragic experience. Senators and Congressmen set aside political differences to pledge themselves to each other and our nation in this time of great need. The world saw their harmonious spirit as they spontaneously broke into patriotic song on the capital steps. Their patriotic spirit overshadowed all political agendas. Truly a transformation of purpose. What did they sing? "God Bless America" of course.

Within days a whole nation was transformed. American patriotism was at the highest level since the attack on Pearl Harbor. American flags sprouted everywhere. One chain of stores reported selling over 500,000 flags within the first week of patriotic transformation. Some stood in lines for hours to buy flags as fast as they were produced. Red, white, and blue became the fashion standard among rich and poor alike.

Within weeks President George W. Bush had the highest approval rate of any president in history. Over 90% of

47

Americans surveyed stood behind him and looked to him for hope and direction. This new president, inaugurated amidst controversy, became the man that the whole world wanted to hear. Other governments, even those not so friendly to Americans, quickly aligned themselves with our new cause.

The transformation was heart-felt. This new wave of transformed feelings swept the globe. The world will wait for the years ahead to evaluate America's leadership and actions. We do not know how long this rejuvenation of direction will last. What we must do, however, is pray that this transformation continues until our goals have been realized and the world becomes a place of peace.

A transformed heart isn't all it will take for our nation to win this war on terrorism, but it helps. It helps a nation. And it helps a church.

Christians must live lives that prove that we have been transformed by our Savior Jesus Christ. Then, through the work of the Holy Spirit within us, we can share our faith so that others may experience the same transformation.

When we study the scriptures we soon realize that not all transformed lives had such an exciting experience as that of the Apostle Paul. For most people transformation begins with the gentle urging of a friend, a co-worker, or a family member who has been transformed. Believers must first care enough about our fellow man and then work with the Holy Spirit to effect eternal change. Power, security, comfort, assurance, endurance, joy and hope are available to everyone everywhere at all times. Tell them now!

Do not conform any longer to the pattern of this world, but be transformed by the renewing of your mind. Then you will be able to test and approve what God's will is—his good, pleasing and perfect will.
Romans 12:2 (NIV)

Chapter 7
"Developing A Heart For Souls"

As Scott settled into his new office at Warner Brothers Studio, he knew he'd arrived professionally but he still had some personal struggles. Scott spent his young adult years as a sound engineer traveling with a rock-n-roll band. Like many others in this profession, he sunk deep into the drug-culture lifestyle.

When he arrived in California to continue his work in the entertainment industry Scott, a Jewish man, began to realize that his past years were wasted in a sinful world and began to seek answers about the meaning of life, particularly his own. He tried several new-age groups and a Guru.

Engel, a co-worker, was living a transformed Christian life before Scott. Engel shared his faith with Scott and assured him that he was praying for Scott to be "saved." Scott didn't know what this term meant but he agreed that he felt "lost....and empty." Engel was not only a Christian, also he truly had a heart for souls. In particular, he had a burden for Scott. Eventually Engel lead Scott to receive Christ and his transformation began.

While listening to Christian radio, Scott decided to call one of the programs to ask for help in finding a reliable church in his area. They referred Scott to First Baptist of Beverly Hills, the church I Pastor. Scott attended and soon made a public profession of faith, was baptized and became an active, ministering member. Among other things, he is the sound engineer for the church, makes visits with me and drives some of the elderly members of the church on their errands.

Scott's story does not end with the transformation of his own life–he's become a transformed witness for Jesus Christ with a deep concern for the souls of others. Scott has shared his experience with co-workers. Some of them mock and ridicule him but Scott remains rooted in his new found faith, church, and family.

Scott's heart for lost souls includes his Jewish mother and siblings. Soon after establishing his relationship to Christ and his church, he took a trip to Florida to visit his family. For Jewish converts the risk of rejection is extremely high. The family took a short cruise off the coast of Florida and at their first dinner aboard the ship, Scott made his announcement. "I have found the Messiah, Jesus Christ." He shared his personal decision and the new direction he had taken. Much to his surprise the family cautiously accepted his testimony. His mother has since visited California and attended a worship service at First Baptist Church. Scott's heart for lost souls continues to grow.

WHY DON'T ALL CHRISTIANS HAVE A HEART FOR LOST SOULS?

Sometimes we bury ourselves in the burden of daily living and lose our joy. The impact of our salvation loses some of its intensity. Scott is a believer of less than one year. He is changing every day. Knowing Jesus is knowing joy for him. He is living a new life. He awakes each morning with a new purpose...he wants everyone to have joy. We need Scott's attitude whether we have known Jesus for days or decades.

Dan is a pastor's son, pastor's brother and a pastor's brother-in-law. He taught Sunday School, sang beautiful solos and led music in his church for many years but he lost his joy when his heart was broken by divorce. He walked away from his church and his Lord.

Two years later he met Laurie. Laurie was raised in a fully dysfunctional family and was twice divorced. Some months later they were married. They attended church only when visiting family. While not against Christianity, she had no desire to pursue a relationship with God that others in the family cherished. The family was well intentioned but vocal about Dan's "backsliding." Everyone showed real concern about Laurie's need for salvation but no one talked about joy.

When Dan's job transferred him to a new community a friend of his father, who was pastor of a local church, made frequent visits to their home. His witnessing added a dimension that others had failed to express. He talked about the joy of salvation. Within a few months a transformation began in Dan and Laurie's lives. Laurie prayed to receive Christ which led to Dan's rededication.

Laurie redecorated the house with religious pictures and verses of Scripture. She took a part-time job in a Christian school and taught Sunday School. Dan returned with a new fervor in music leadership and performances. They have two children who join them in joyful worship. The joy of salvation was renewed in Dan's life and added to Laurie's.

Laurie's question for the family was simple to ask but difficult to answer. "Why didn't someone tell me about the joy of knowing Jesus sooner?"

How can we bring about a transformation of Christians to develop a heart for lost souls?

SHARE THE JOY

Joseph, a 12-year-old boy from Egypt is from a Muslim family. His immediate family, on his mother's side, lives in Italy but Joseph came to southeastern Arkansas to visit his Anglo grandmother one summer. His first experience with the Christian faith came in Vacation Bible School in a small country church alongside Lake Chicot.

Joseph enjoyed the entire week long experience . He loved the Bible stories, the crafts, and memorizing scriptures. What impressed him the most was what he saw in the lives of his teachers Ray and Susan. He saw their joy! Ray, a long time Christian, had drifted away from active service to God until rededicating his life four years earlier. His wife also had a refreshing of her faith in becoming a Baptist after token years in the Lutheran faith of her family. The transformation in their lives was now clearly seen as the joy of salvation was shared with their small Vacation Bible School class. The impact would reach the other side of the world.

Three weeks after Bible School, Joseph's mother called the church from Italy. She had many concerns about the impact of the World Trade Center explosions on the life of her family. She did not complain that Joseph had been in a Christian environment. She was not the least bit upset over her son coming to Christ. She saw the joy of salvation in her son's life. A true transformation had taken place. She expressed her thanks to the church for the new Hope Joseph found and the joy he expressed.

Two weeks after the mother's call came word from Joseph's college age sisters. Both young women are students at a school about 300 miles north. They were making plans to visit grandma Steena in the near future. This time they were coming with a purpose. "We want what Joseph has in his life." What impressed them was the joy of salvation.

THE JOY OF ASSURANCE

My wife and I recently took a trip to Arkansas to visit friends. The Los Angeles to Dallas leg of the trip went through a severe thunderstorm. The turbulence was more violent than we had ever experienced. We lost 3000 feet of altitude in just seconds. The shaking produced many expressions of fear followed by complete silence. The pilot ordered everyone to the nearest empty seat rather than returning to their own. A flight attendant sat across the aisle from us and strapped herself down. Next to my wife was a first-time flyer. Needless to say she was somewhat panicked. She wanted to hear words of assurance of a safe landing. The flight attendant expressed her own concerns by announcing to our troubled fellow passengers that it was her worst experience in 11½ years of flying! She had no words of assurance. Her own fear overwhelmed her.

52

We all seek assurance during trying times. We want comfort when we are afraid. In all areas of life, we want to hear words that assure us of our well being. We want to hear confident words and see fearless acts. We want to feel that all will be well. Can we be assured?

The only assurance that we have in this life comes from God. The assurance of eternal life is available for the future but begins with our present. When we accept Christ we become 'sons.' Sometimes our disobedience may bring His chastening but we remain 'sons' of a loving omnipotent Father. His power exceeds any threat that man may pose

"And this is the testimony: God has given us eternal life, and this life is in his Son. ¹²He who has the Son has life; he who does not have the Son of God does not have life." (1 John 5:11-12 NIV)

JOY OF INTRODUCING

Some years ago, I was relaxing in my bathtub when the door opened and I was greeted by my 4-year-old daughter holding the hand of her playmate, a 3-year-old neighbor boy. She was so happy to introduce her friend to me that she could not wait until my bath was over.

We all enjoy introducing our friends to others. The greatest joy comes when we introduce our friends to our closest friend, Jesus.

As we study the New Testament we are quick to realize that there are twelve disciples. Just as quickly we see that the focus of the Scripture centers around only two or three of these followers of our Lord. One of those, Andrew, receives little attention. When mentioned at all he is identified as "Peter's brother." Peter of course, the spokesman for the twelve, is featured in scripture most frequently of all. Most of us would be unhappy if our only significance was that we are "somebody's brother." But Andrew may have had the most joy of all.

Andrew is nicknamed by many as "the introducer." The Gospel of John records several events in the life of this little mentioned disciple. John 1:40-42 tells us that Andrew was one of the first disciples to answer Christ's call and his first action was to seek out his brother, Simon Peter, and introduce him to Jesus. Simon may get all the attention, but it was Andrew who brought him to the Lord.

In John 6:1-15 the story of Jesus feeding 5,000 is recorded. We emphasize the miracle of feeding such a number with the lunch of a small boy. We all remember the event and the boy but most overlook verses 8-9 which tell us that it was Andrew who introduced the boy to Jesus.

In John 12:20-22 Andrew once again is seen introducing someone to Jesus. This time it was Greek worshipers who came to the Passover feast. In the glow of the triumphant entry and the shadow of the crucifixion stood Andrew. As we stand in the darkness of a lost world we must remember we are reflections of the resurrection. The questions that we must answer are these:

- Do I express the joy of my salvation in front of the people I encounter?
- Does the witness I present in my life reflect the assurance of salvation?
- Am I an introducer?
  - Who have I introduced to Jesus?
  - Who can I introduce to Jesus?
  - Who will I introduce to Jesus?

Chapter 8
"Developing A Heart For Evangelism"

My first pastorate was at an American Indian Mission in Los Angeles County. During my four years of service to this congregation I learned more and developed much more than the congregation did. They knew more about being a church than I knew about leading one. With less than 10 sermons preached I entered an arena that would transform my own life. I knew how to buy Bibles and tracts and even the mechanics of leading someone to Christ. What I did not have was a heart for Evangelism. By the time I left the church four years later, I had begun to develop a heart for evangelism. Leon, a reformed alcoholic, taught his pastor to witness.

Leon's two passions in life were drinking at an "Indian bar" and fighting. He was proficient at both. He stood about six foot, four inches tall, had a rugged build, and a face that carried the scars of some battles he had lost and maybe even some that he had won.

Leon's cousin came into his life while he was as low as an alcoholic could be. The cousin, a new Christian, shared with Leon the joy of his salvation and soon Leon found Christ as well. He not only received salvation through the witness of this cousin, he also received a transformed heart. He began to develop a real heart for evangelism.

When I arrived on the scene, Leon was eager to learn more about evangelism from his new pastor. He could not wait to make evangelistic visits with the new leader of his church. Then came our first opportunity to step into the living room of an American-Indian couple we had heard moved near the church. With Bibles, tracts, and prayers at the ready, we knocked on the door of the couple's tiny home. Much to my surprise they invited us in. The young man sat with us in the living room while his wife continued with her clean-up chores in the kitchen.

I began to small talk with Abraham. We talked about our likes and dislikes, jobs, weather and sports. We did not even mention Jesus during the first 30 minutes. Abraham and I did most of the talking while a frustrated Leon looked on. Then came Leon's embarrassing question. "Pastor, didn't we come here for you to tell this man about Jesus?" (A subject I had clearly avoided.)

I changed the direction of our conversation soon after Leon's interruption. I fumbled, stammered but finally was able to share the plan of salvation with an attentive young man. With a shaking voice and knees to match, I asked him if he wanted to pray to receive Jesus as his Savior. He thought about it for a while with his head hanging silently. He lifted his head slowly and said "no, but thank you for stopping by."

In the silence that followed came a heart transforming moment. Mary, Abraham's wife, had completed her work in the kitchen and was standing in the doorway listening to my feeble presentation. With a quiet voice she said, "I do." She entered the room and Leon shared his personal testimony I had the privilege of leading Mary in the prayer to receive Jesus Christ as Savior. What a joyous victory for Christ in spite of my personal failings.

Later that night I received my second lesson from Leon, concerning a heart for evangelism. He told me about the time he wore a red ribbon on his shirt for Jesus. He had been trained during the "Good News Campaign" of the late sixties. One of the suggested methods for gaining witnessing opportunities was the wearing of a small red ribbon on your shirt or jacket. Leon thought it was a great way to open the door to sharing his faith with five other car pool members on their way to work on Monday morning. Leon wore the ribbon but no one asked why. The second and third days passed yet no one asked why he wore the ribbon. On day four Leon wore a much larger ribbon but again no response. On Friday he wore the ribbon again but was not willing to be ignored this time. As he entered the car he blurted out, "Don't you see this ribbon I'm wearing and don't you want to know why?" Without hesitation Leon shared his testimony, presented the Gospel and two co-workers came to know Jesus.

Leon gave me a great gift while I was his Pastor, he gave me the awareness of my need for an evangelistic heart. I saw the transformed life of an alcoholic develop a fervor for sharing the same faith that set him free from the bondage of sin. I also learned the importance of not only having a heart for evangelism but of also sharing that heart with others as Leon did with me.

HELPING OTHERS DISCOVER THEIR EVANGELISTIC HEART

My phone rang at 3:00 in the morning. To my surprise it wasn't a church member in need, but rather a concerned mother and grandmother whom I had never met. After many apologies she told me about her son, David, his wife Amy, and two young children. She had found my name in the yellow pages and made the call in spite of the hour. Her son had been raised in a Christian home in Bakersfield. He had become successful in owning two restaurants on the north east part of San Francisco Bay. Both made the family a lot of money but quickly led to alcohol and drug abuse. Grandma was deeply concerned about her son and daughter-in-law but even more the two children who had never been to church. I listened to a grandmother's broken heart–a heart broken by a son who had chosen to turn away from his commitment to Christ. I agreed to visit in the home that evening.

I called Gary and shared the story and invited him to make the visit with me. We were greeted warmly at the door to a beautiful home. Soon David arrived from the restaurant to meet with us. We shared Christ and our personal testimonies but we were not sure of the results God would bring. David soon excused himself to return to work. His only commitment was to consider a visit to our church in the near future. I could see on Amy's face a greater concern for herself and the children. Sensing the need in her life, I asked grandma to take the children out of the room for a few minutes. Soon after, Amy gave her heart to Christ and then immediately shared the news with her mother-in-law in the next room. They returned and we all rejoiced in what God did. It was Gary's first time to be involved in leading someone to Jesus.

We exchanged hugs with the family and headed for home. We turned the first corner and Gary pulled the car to the curb and stopped abruptly. Without saying a word he leaped from the car, stood between the headlights, jumped straight in the air and clicked his heels together. Gary had just received the first blessing that comes to those with an evangelistic heart.

EVANGELISTIC HEARTS
PRODUCE EVANGELISTIC RESULTS

Gary was excited. Amy's decision was genuine and was soon made public and followed by believer's baptism. It did not stop with one or two evangelistic experiences but continued in Gary's life for many years.

Gary's development of an evangelistic heart spread to others in the church as well. It only takes one or two in a church to encourage others in to share their faith. That year a church averaging just over 100 in attendance baptized fifty people–mostly young adults.

Evangelistic hearts produce evangelistic churches and when our focus is upon the needs of the unsaved rather than upon ourselves, joy increases. Abundant joy is the evidence of an evangelistic heart.

WHEN EVANGELISTIC HEARTS FADE

After four rewarding years in an evangelistic church, I accepted the call to a church that I thought would provide greater opportunities for personal growth. The challenge was much greater than I anticipated. I soon found myself trapped in an administrative prison. Keeping peace and making budgets while leading a church and Christian school was at times overwhelming. The church itself was self-sufficient and saw little need for evangelistic efforts. They were good people who loved their church, but sharing their faith was not on the agenda. Churches quickly become stale and indifferent when an evangelistic effort is not prevalent.

Campus Crusade for Christ invited me to attend their first seminar on Discipleship. I went hoping that it would inspire me and help me inspire the congregation. The first two days focused on the discipleship program. I saw no way to make use of their program at my church.

On the third day we were told that we would be trained in the use of the "Four Spiritual Laws" tract. This tract had been the central focus of Campus Crusade ministries for many years. My training partner that day was a pastor of a Nazarene Church in the same city. We eagerly did the role play and found ourselves competing with each other in our "mock-witnessing" efforts. Then came the field assignment–telephone evangelism. We were assigned to a cubical with two phones, one for the person sharing the Gospel, one for the observer. Our prospect list was nothing more than a page from the phone book. We were given two hours to complete the task.

Fifteen minutes went by without making one call. Pastor David and I were locked in a debate on who would make the first call. Neither of us had done this before and neither wanted to start at that moment. He finally prevailed by reminding me of how evangelistic Baptists, claim to be. He shamed me into the first call.

The phone rang several times, then was answered by a 17-year-old high school student just in from school. I made the introduction and then began to share my testimony and quickly moved to a Gospel presentation using the "Four Spiritual Laws." The teenager, much to our surprise, listened intently. He then, to our greater surprise, prayed to receive Jesus Christ as his Savior. Fortunately I knew a pastor in his neighborhood and made a referral. The mood in our cubicle changed. Pastor David was eager to share. When our time was up, we both thanked God for the one who came to know Christ. We realized it was truly the work of the Holy Spirt and not because of either of the reluctant witnesses. On my return home I called the pastor and related the event to him. He told me that young man had already called the church and was meeting with the youth group that evening.

Hearts change when we witness. You may realize that the greatest change may occur in the witness rather than the prospect. We may continue to be changed by coming beside fellow Christians who are more experienced and comfortable in sharing their faith. We learn from each other and our heart for evangelism grows.

Chapter 9
"Developing A Heart For
Evangelistic Opportunities"

When is the right time to share your faith? For many Christians the answer is never. Others may find that the right time is only when asked. There are some Christians who have a "Heart For Evangelistic Opportunities" and are always ready. The question is what does God want?

Peter puts it this way: ". . . In your hearts set apart Christ as Lord. Always be prepared to give an answer to everyone who asks you to give a reason for the hope that you have. But do this with gentleness and respect, keeping a clear conscience, so that those who speak maliciously against your good behavior in Christ may be ashamed of their slander." (1 Peter 3:15-16 NIV)

Having the heart for evangelistic opportunities means that you know the right time to share the Gospel. Some think the right time is 11:00 a.m. on Sunday and the right person to share the Gospel is the pastor. Others might be willing for Sunday School teachers at 9:45 a.m. to be the right person, at the right time and in the right place.

A person with a heart for evangelistic opportunities is always prepared to share his faith. He is convinced that the right time is now, the right place is here, and the right person to share is me.

Ray and Sue came to know Christ in the hospital room the evening their first son was born. A young boy in Rialto found Christ through a phone call after a day at school. Amy found the Lord in her living room while Mary came to Christ from the kitchen door. Church altars and classrooms are not the only places that God reaches people for the kingdom.

The person with a "heart for evangelistic opportunities" knows the right candidate for evangelism. At this point far too often we fail to see our opportunities because we exclude so many from our "evangelistic candidate" list. Some we encounter may be too rich or too poor. Others too old or too young. Still others may be so far away from the Christian life that we are sure they cannot be reached. Those with hearts for evangelistic opportunities know that anyone who does not have a saving relationship with Christ is the right candidate.

The fifth element in an evangelistic opportunity is the working of the right spirit. Some evangelistic attempts fail because we are witnessing in our own spirit rather than in the Spirit of God. Evangelistic opportunities arise when we are following the direction the Holy Spirit gives. We must remember that it is the Holy Spirit that convicts of sin. The Apostle Paul wrote:

"What, after all, is Apollos? And what is Paul? Only servants, through whom you came to believe—as the Lord has assigned to each his task. [6]I planted the seed, Apollos watered it, but God made it grow. [7]So neither he who plants nor he who waters is anything, but only God, who makes things grow. [8]The man who plants and the man who waters have one purpose, and each will be rewarded according to his own labor. [9]For we are God's fellow workers; you are God's field, God's building." (1 Corinthians 3:5-9 NIV)

HUBERT

Hubert's brother called the church office mid-day on Saturday. Gary, my co-trainer in Parakaleo Ministries, and I were hard at work preparing for an upcoming conference on deacon ministry. The call reminded me of many others I had received. "My brother Hubert is in intensive care at a hospital near your church. I am concerned since he is the only family member who does not know Christ. His condition is extremely serious, he has lung cancer. Will you come and share Christ with him?" I put the man on hold and spoke with my co-trainer. Our choices were simple. I can tell him we can't make it today because of our busy schedule or we can put our work on hold and make the visit. We prayed and decided we had to make the visit or forfeit the right to teach others about ministry. I let him know that we were on our way.

Hubert's brother greeted us in the hallway. He filled us in on his rebellious brother, now in his mid fifties. He left the family at 18, vowing to make it rich in the oil fields of Signal Hill (Long Beach) California and to never again attend church. He kept both vows.

I reminded myself of the many similar visits I had made to the same hospital. I had heard similar stories from relatives or friends. I also remembered that on all previous occasions the one I would visit was not receptive, several times they were even hostile. Gary and I prayed with Hubert's brother and somehow we all knew this visit would be different. We entered the room.

Hubert's brother made the introductions and I sat next to Hubert. We shared our likes, dislikes and concerns for the future. After a few moments I asked Hubert to tell me about his relationship to God. He freely responded. He talked about being in church every service. About his anger toward his parents for forcing him to go. He told me of his vow to never return to church as soon as he turned eighteen.

My second question was the same as the first. I reminded him that I asked him to tell me about his relationship to God not his relationship to the church. He began to cry. He didn't have a relationship with God. I shared how he could begin that relationship immediately. After hearing God's plan of salvation Hubert prayed and received Christ. He was ready now to talk about church.

Hubert's lung cancer went into remission. I referred him

to a church in Lakewood whose pastor was also in a serious stage of progressive lung cancer. Hubert made a public profession and was baptized. He attended faithfully and gave financially on a regular basis. Hubert's brother went back to New Mexico. Deacons were trained, and the angels in Heaven rejoiced.

Right place. Right time. Right candidate. Right spirit. Right person, sharing the right message.

ERIC

Chris is a mortician and ordained minister. In 1997, Chris' funeral home purchased another across town. Eric, one of the two morticians there, actually lived on top of the funeral home for eighteen years. Eric is 6'3' and weighs about 240lbs. He is an ex-professional baseball player–very loud, obnoxious and arrogant.

Eric was a crude and worldly man. He came from an abusive family and has been an alcoholic since he was a teenager. Chris knew that working with him on a daily basis was going to be difficult.

Eric noticed that Chris was different. Chris told him he was a Christian. "That's fine for you," Eric said, "but don't go preaching any of that Christian [expletive deleted] to me." Chris said, "I decided to put him on my prayer list. I thought *OK God, let's see what you can do!*"

As time went by, Eric had real battles with his alcoholism. He finally got to the point where he went into a clinic to get cleaned up. His job was on the line and he knew he had to do something. He was gone for a month. Upon his return he apologized to everyone and was ready to work and stay away from the alcohol. The program told him he needed a spiritual focus to help him combat his alcoholism. Chris tried to tell him at that time what a relationship with Christ was and how God could change his life. He still didn't want any part of it and quickly shut Chris down by claiming that the spiritual focus could be anything or anyone. He didn't want Jesus and

Jesus wouldn't want him. He had done "too many rotten things."

Chris ached, wanting Eric to listen to the Gospel. Eric stayed clean for a year. Then he had a relapse. Eric told Chris that he had started drinking again and was not sure what to do. Again, Chris told him where he could start. Once again, Eric ended the conversation, not wanting to hear about Jesus.

In May 2001, Chris prayed faithfully every day for at least 6 weeks for some of his friends and family members to be saved. Eric was one of the people on his list. Chris prayed for Eric faithfully, not missing a single day, for 8 weeks. The praying did not change Eric much but it did change Chris. He became more sensitive to opportunities to witness to Eric because Eric was specifically on his mind. Chris was on a mission!

In the 8th week, Chris arrived at work and was met at the door by his boss, a non-believer. "Chris, you need to get over to Eric, he is at home not doing good. I think he needs God and I figured you are the one to go visit him."

Chris went to the funeral home where Eric lives and knocked on the door. He heard a very feeble, "the door is open." Eric was still in his pajamas and looked very depressed. He would not look at Chris, instead he just stared straight ahead. "What's going on?" Chris asked. "I don't know," Eric said, "my life is a mess and I don't know what to do."

"How can I help?" Chris asked. Eric responded, "For the past four years I have watched you and your family and I've noticed that you have a peace and joy that I have never had." Then he said, "I want it."

"The answer is simple," Chris said, "You need Jesus." Finally Eric said "Tell me about Jesus." For the next hour he sat and listened, there was none of the sarcasm, jokes, or teasing that Chris had become so accustomed to hearing from Eric. When Chris finished giving the plan of Salvation Eric said, "I want Jesus in my life!"

Today, Eric is a different person. The crudeness is almost gone and when it does show Eric expresses remorse. His language is cleaner. He has read through the entire New Testament and has been faithful at church.

As Chris baptized him, Eric whispered in his ear two simple words-- "thank you."

SONNY

Sonny's transformation came during a period of deep tragedy. Christy, his wife of less than a year suffered a fatal stroke just two weeks after the birth of their much wanted child. Christy professed and lived a close relationship to God through Jesus Christ. Sonny was a good son of Christian parents but he had chosen to live outside the faith. Shortly after their marriage a deacon in Sonny's parents' church provided some basic marriage counseling for this young couple. A relationship between the deacon, Sonny and Christy grew through the months.

Sonny and Christy spent many hours together at the local stock car track. Sonny and his family built cars and drove in the Nevada Race Circuit. Much of what Sonny knew about life came from the pits. This is not the best place to learn morals–most of the racing community have little time for God.

Early Monday morning, after a weekend at the track, Christy suffered a brain aneurysm. For all practical purposes her 21-year-old life ended that morning. In the emergency room her bodily functions were kept in motion by the life-support equipment. About 3:00 p.m. the neurosurgeon explained that the brain damage was irreversible and Christy would not survive. The family would need to make a decision to remove the life-support systems and allow for her death.

In the waiting room, nearly fifty people came to pray and support Sonny and the rest of the family. Pastor Mike,

Christy's deacon and many others from the church were joined by an equal number of Sonny's friends from the track. They talked, prayed and expressed hope.

The doctor asked Sonny to approve the donation of Christy's organs. He agreed. (A few weeks later a letter of thanks from the Nevada Organ Transplant Institute arrived. Sixty people benefitted from the donation of Christy's organs.)

When the doctors left the room, Sonny and the deacon had time to talk. After prayer, the concerned deacon shared the one thing Christy would have wanted most, the transplant of her faith to her unsaved husband. After hearing the Gospel presented in such a delicate situation Sonny prayed to receive Christ. He left the room, went directly to his mother and announced, "Mom, I now have the Lord in my heart, we can get through even this."

On December 9, Kylie, a 4-month-old child was dedicated to the Lord by her Christian father. It would have been Christy's 22nd birthday.

Sonny's story has not ended. He has been faithful in church and personal study since coming to know the Lord. Several other "race track" friends have also been attending Sonny's church. The witness of God at work will certainly touch many lives for the kingdom.

The day before Christy's aneurysm, Sonny's parents stopped at In-And-Out Burger for lunch. A friend pointed out a scripture on the bottom of the cup, Nahum 1:7. During the long hours in the hospital that followed their deacon shared this same passage with them. It says,

"The Lord is good, a refuge in times of trouble. He cares for those who trust in Him." Nahum 1:7

Section III: Transformed Witness
by Randy McWhorter

Chapter 10
"Saved For A Reason; Not Just A Season"

W hen you were saved, God did not clean you up: He cleaned you out. God is not just interested in your reform, or your recovery; He transforms every aspect of the life surrendered to Him. The Bible is clear about the change in one's life that happens at the point of salvation: "If any one is in Christ, he is a new creation. The old has gone and everything has been made new." (2 Corinthians 5:17) Wow! That is transformation. Every Christian has new life in Christ.

Now what? What does God expect us to do with this new life? Of course, He wants us to live for Him. He wants our lives to be different. He wants us to love Him and worship Him.

However, if all God desired out of salvation was fellowship with Him why does He leave us here on earth after He saves us? It would certainly be best for us if God were to take us to heaven the moment we are saved. Think of it. We would not have to struggle with temptation to sin because there is no temptation in heaven. We would not have to live in the pollution of sin in the world. We would not have to suffer pain, illness, or worry about money, food and life's necessities. Sorrow could not touch us. We would never again experience disappointment or discouragement. Why does God leave us here on earth after we have been transformed?

The Apostle Paul wrestled with this truth in Philippians 1:22-24, "If I am to go on living in the body, this will mean fruitful labor for me. Yet what shall I choose? I do not know! I am torn between the two: I desire to depart and be with Christ, which is better by far; but it is more necessary for you that I remain in the body."

There is only one reason we remain on earth while we wait to spend eternity with Jesus in heaven. It is the reason that ought to bring focus to every aspect of our lives. It is the goal that ought to captivate our best efforts. God leaves those who have been saved on earth in order to share with those who have not been saved how they can get to heaven. We have been saved and left on earth not just for a season but also for a reason.

YOU HAVE THE POWER

The Apostle Paul urged the church in Corinth that they not receive God's grace in vain (2 Corinthians 6:1). How would one do that? He goes on to say, "now is the time of God's favor, now is the day of salvation." (2 Corinthians 6:2) He is saying that we need to make the most of the time we have here on earth. To live our lives without realizing the urgency of sharing the message of salvation with those who need to hear it would be to live your life here on earth in vain.

We are transformed witnesses of God's love and grace. Our lives were made new in Christ and now, we are to be agents of transformation in the lives of others. The Bible is clear about God's insistence that we be witnesses. Acts 1:8 records the last earthly words of Jesus, "But you will receive power when the Holy Spirit comes on you; and you will be my witnesses in Jerusalem, and in all Judea and Samaria, and to the ends of the earth."

This verse reveals the promise of power for witnessing. Our transformations came complete with the power to accomplish the purpose for which we have been left on earth. We have the Holy Spirit's power that enables us to fulfill our commission from God.

69

Simultaneous with the salvation experience is the baptism of the Holy Spirit. This is what Acts 1:8 refers to as "when the Holy Spirit comes upon you." This baptism brings the continual presence of God's Spirit that dwells within every believer. Every Christian, because of the Spirit's indwelling, is given a spiritual gift that is to be used in witnessing to others. Spiritual gifts are Divine assistance for witnessing. Darrell Robinson in his book, Total Church Life, says, "God has gifted all members with all that is necessary for them to fulfill their God-given ministry." (page 93)

LIFE UNDER THE INFLUENCE

There is a difference between the baptism of the Holy Spirit and the filling of the Holy Spirit. The baptism of the Holy Spirit is a one-time, never repeated, experience. The filling is best explained as being under the control or influence of the Holy Spirit. Ephesians 5:18 captures this understanding, "Do not get drunk on wine, which leads to debauchery. Instead, be filled with the Spirit."

Being filled with the Holy Spirit requires an effort on the part of the believer. Though we continually possess the Holy Spirit, we are not filled with the Holy Spirit at all times. The reason we are not filled at all times is because we do not allow the Holy Spirit to control us all of the time. Sometimes we are filled with anger, or filled with pride or filled with something else–during those times, we are not Spirit-filled. Power for witnessing requires that we be filled with the Holy Spirit.

To be filled with the Holy Spirit one must have a desire to be Spirit-filled. Romans 8:5-6 says, "Those who live according to the sinful nature have their minds set on what that nature desires; but those who live in accordance with the Spirit have their minds set on what the Spirit desires. The mind of sinful man is death, but the mind controlled by the Spirit is life and peace." The desire of every witness is to please God. This desire is primarily centered in our thought life. To be filled with the Holy Spirit we need to have our minds "set on what the Spirit desires."

So, what does the Spirit desire? The Spirit desires you to develop a Christ-like character. The Christian with the desire will be given the power to develop what Galatians 5:22-23 calls "the fruit of the Spirit." The Spirit also desires to lead you to obey Jesus. 1 Peter 1:2 gives us this insight as it refers to those to whom the book was written. It is written to those, "who have been chosen according to the foreknowledge of God the Father, through the sanctifying work of the Spirit, for obedience to Jesus Christ ..." The power of the Spirit enables the Christian to live in obedience.

To be filled with the Spirit one must be devoted. The Apostle Paul was concerned for the Christians in Corinth, in 2 Corinthians 11:3 he wrote, "But I am afraid that just as Eve was deceived by the serpent's cunning, your minds may somehow be led astray from your sincere and pure devotion to Christ." Again, the place where this devotion is centered is in "your minds." Without devotion to Christ we can not fulfill the Spirit's desires.

To be filled with the Spirit, one must make a decision to be filled. Ephesians 5:18 issues this command, "Do not get drunk on wine, which leads to debauchery. Instead, be filled with the Spirit." Just as you would decide to take the drink of wine and get drunk, you must decide to allow yourself to be under the control of the Spirit.

The person who wants to be filled with the Holy Spirit needs a sincere longing (desire), a separated life (devotion), and a settled loyalty (decision). When we are filled with the Holy Spirit, evangelism becomes natural. When you are filled with the Holy Spirit there is a power that gives you boldness to speak to others about Jesus.

THE BOLD AND THE BEAUTIFUL

The first century Christians were bold witnesses. When Jesus promised the Holy Spirit would come upon them, He

71

also said there would be power. There was a specific reason for the power; to be witnesses everywhere. Somewhere in the last couple of millenniums Christians have confused the purpose of the Spirit's power from being His bold witnesses to being His blessing recipients. We have believed the Spirit's power in us is to help make our lives more comfortable and easy rather than to fight the spiritual forces that would seek to prevent the truth of the gospel from being shared and accepted.

Every time the book of Acts mentions the filling of the Spirit it also speaks of sharing the gospel with boldness. The day of Pentecost, recorded in Acts 2, says, "... and they were all filled with the Holy Spirit and began to speak with other tongues, as the Spirit gave them utterance." (verse 4) The speaking in tongues mentioned here is not a selfish prayer language but was the ability to communicate the gospel in an unknown dialect. It was obviously more than just a sign that the Holy Spirit had come as promised; it was a powerful filling that enabled the Disciples to boldly share the gospel. The filling of the Spirit made them bold witnesses. It certainly did not make life easier for them.

Again, in Acts 4, Peter was filled with the Spirit and began to boldly share the gospel to hostile people. The filling of the Holy Spirit did not make life more comfortable for the Apostle but it did give him boldness to witness for the Lord in the face of persecution.

In Acts 4:31 there is another mention of the Spirit's filling. After the believers prayed for boldness to share the gospel it says, "... and they were all filled with the Holy Spirit, and began to speak the word of God with boldness."

Stephen, the first Christian martyr, was full of the Spirit's power. His witness cost him his life. (see Acts 7:59) Philip, a first century Christian, was under the influence of the Spirit and boldly witnessed to an Ethiopian. (See Acts 8:26-40) Paul, the transformed persecutor of the Church, witnessed boldly after being filled with the Holy Spirit. (See Acts

13:9ff)

The thrill of the fill is not power to live a life of luxury but, rather, to live an obedient life of witnessing. Many today are more concerned with the Spirit's power to add quality to their lives than the power to be a bold witness. The bold witness is a thing of beauty to our Lord. That's why it says in Romans 10:15, "... How beautiful are the feet of them that preach the gospel of peace, and bring glad tidings of good things!" The bold are the beautiful. The filled are the fairest. Those who witness are wonderful. The gospel sharers are gorgeous saints!

Chapter 11
"A Plan For Bold Witnessing"

A PLAN FOR ALL SEASONS

Peter wrote, "Be ready to give a reason for the hope that lies in you." (1 Peter 3:18) The Bible is clear when it comes to our command to be witnesses. Peter says that we are to be ready to share the hope. In order to be ready we need to be prepared when the opportunities to share present themselves. This means that we must give attention to the method we'll use in witnessing.

Not every witnessing situation is the same. Opportunities to share the hope are numerous and varied. Some situations are spur-of-the-moment opportunities. Others are premeditated. Some encounters are long discussions, while others are brief and never repeated opportunities.

The obedient witness prepares to share the hope in any situation. There are many resources available to assist in this preparation. However, preparation alone will not provide the power for witnessing. As already stated, the filling of the Holy Spirit will enable anyone who has been transformed to share the good news. All that is really needed to be a witness is the willingness to tell the story of what God has done in your life.

Your story is a powerful tool for witnessing. The essence of witnessing is in the willingness to tell what has happened. Many Christians mistake the command to be witnesses as a command to be salespersons. Some think that we must make a clever presentation in order to coerce those who do not believe in Jesus that they want and need to make a decision. Some Christians mistake the command to be witnesses as a request to practice law. Like a lawyer, some Christians believe that they must argue people into the Kingdom. But in reality God has not commanded us to be in sales or law; He has commanded us to be His witnesses. He wants you to tell what you know.

Preparation to share the hope that lies in us begins with the desire, dedication, and decision to be obedient to Jesus Christ. This will ensure that one is filled with the Spirit and has the power to be a witness. The next step in preparation concerns the way in which the witness shares the good news. Being ready to share the hope means we must prepare for all situations that may arise that give us an opportunity to witness. This means we should have a plan that will assist us to be effective in our sharing.

TELL THEM A STORY

The story of what God has done in your life will be your most valuable asset in witnessing. Preparation for witnessing should include using your story in such a way so as to communicate most effectively the transformation that has taken place in your life.

As you prepare your story to be an effective witnessing tool, it would be good to see how others have used their story in witnessing encounters. Paul, in Acts 26:9-23 uses his story to witness to King Agrippa. A woman from Samaria, in John 4:39ff uses her story to witness to the whole town. Both of these testimonies contain common characteristics that give us help in preparing our story. In both instances care was given to include information that would assist the hearers to understand the transformation that had taken place.

As you prepare to share your story, study the way Paul and the woman from Samaria told theirs'. There are three main elements that guided their presentations. The first was centered on the story of their life before they had accepted Jesus Christ as their Lord and Savior. Paul talked about how he was a persecutor of the Church. The woman from Samaria spoke of how Jesus knew everything she had ever done. In both of these examples, the simple truth of life before the transformation made by accepting Christ was presented clearly and without elaboration.

The second element present in both stories is brief explanation of how they came to know of their need and how they committed their lives to Christ. Paul had a dramatic experience on the road to Damascus that transformed his life forever. The woman from Samaria met the true Messiah and He transformed her. In order to be effective when we have the opportunity to share our story we need to be clear about the transformation in our life.

The last common element of the woman from Samaria and Paul's stories centers on what God has done and is doing in their lives. The woman from Samaria said, "we know that this man really is the Savior of the world." Paul was more specific and shared that he, "obtained help from God and has become a witness to both the small and the great." Both were simply telling how God helps them in their daily lives.

As you prepare to share the hope that lies in you give attention to these three elements. Tell the story of your life before you came to know Jesus in a personal way. Share the truth of how you came to realize your need for Jesus and how you made your commitment to Him. And then, include the way in which Jesus makes a difference in your life today. This simple outline aide will ensure that you include everything necessary to communicate your story effectively.

THE POWER OF THE GOSPEL

At some point in the witnessing experience it will be necessary to share the gospel. "Gospel" is a word that the Bible uses to refer to the life, death, and resurrection of Jesus Christ. John Mark, the writer of the book of Mark, refers to the content contained in the book as "the gospel of Jesus Christ, the Son of God."(Mark 1:1) Paul, in Romans 1:16 informs us that he is, "not ashamed of the gospel of Christ:

for it is the power of God unto salvation to everyone that believes; to the Jew first, and also to the Greek." In 1 Timothy 1:10, Paul says that God has, "brought life and immortality to light through the gospel." When we were made new in Christ the gospel was shared with us at some time. All Christians have heard, believed, and received the gospel message. It is the only way to be saved. 1 Corinthians 1:18 says that, "... the preaching of the cross is to those that are perishing foolishness, but to us that are saved it is the power of God." God's power to save a person is contained in the gospel.

This single fact makes the gospel message we are commanded to share controversial and confrontational. It is controversial because it is exclusive. It is confrontational because a decision must be made. The only way of salvation is belief in the gospel of Jesus Christ. Jesus sealed the exclusivity of salvation in these words, "I am the way, the truth, and the life. No one goes to the Father but by Me." (John 14:6) The gospel is exclusive in its requirement for salvation but it is inclusive in the realm of opportunity. Romans 1:13 gives the broad scope of salvations' opportunity, "Whoever calls on the name of the Lord will be saved." Everyone is given the opportunity to accept the gospel (inclusive) but only those who in faith believe and accept the gospel are saved (exclusive).

The gospel is neither hard to understand nor hard to share. When sharing the gospel do not be duped by the devil into believing that it is too difficult for someone to understand. It may be difficult for people to believe the gospel but it is not difficult to understand. The Bible simply tells us the gospel as a matter of fact. 1 Corinthians 15:3-4 is the gospel in a nutshell: "... how that Christ died for our sins according to the scriptures; And that he was buried, and that he rose again the third day according to the scriptures." The gospel is not a theory to debate; it is a truth to declare. Remember that God has not commanded us to be salesmen or lawyers but witnesses. And even though we did not see the life, death, or resurrection of Jesus (which is the gospel we are to witness), we have experienced the power of the gospel in our lives. Our lives were transformed when we heard of, believed in, and received Jesus as our Lord and Savior. We are witnesses of the gospel's power to transform a life.

You will want to make sure that you share the gospel as you tell your story. Include how you came to hear about Jesus and how you accepted Him as your personal Lord and Savior. People will want to know what it is that made the difference in your life. Tell them the truth, the whole truth. Tell them about the time you were apart from Christ. Tell them that one day you heard that God loved you enough to send Jesus, His only Son, to die on the cross in order to save you from the penalty of your sin. Tell them how you believed that Jesus died on the cross for you and that He was buried and that on the third day He rose from the dead. Tell them that Jesus is making a difference in your life today by giving you a purpose for living and help along the way. Tell them, because the gospel has the power to transform any life. Even theirs.

THE MOST AWKWARD MOMENT IN LIFE

Sharers of the gospel are not immune from feelings of fear, embarrassment, or doubt. The most awkward moment of any witnessing experience is at the point of asking for a decision. That moment is often dreaded and avoided. We dread putting other people on the spot. We avoid any conversation that may be confrontational or even controversial. It is easier to simply share our story and quit. But is that what God wants us to do? Is that what people who have not experienced life in Christ need us to do?

Any time you have the opportunity to share your story you are planting the gospel seed in a heart. Sometimes, as you begin to share what Jesus has done for you, the person with whom you are sharing has already heard the gospel. In that case you could be said to be watering the seed that someone else has already planted. But there are those occasions when the seed has been planted and watered and now is the time for harvest. The Spirit-filled witness will be sensitive at the point of decision to know what stage of readiness the person they are witnessing to is in.

Assumptions must not prevent you from asking the person you have been sharing with if they would like to know how Christ could transform their life. Never assume that a person is not ready to receive the gospel. In fact, if you must assume something, assume that they are ready to make a decision until you receive a clear confirmation that you have shared enough.

There are many ways in which a witness can initiate the opportunity for a person to make a decision for Christ. One of the most natural transitions from sharing your story (which includes the gospel) to asking for a decision is by asking the simple question, "Has anything like that ever happened to you?" The answer to that simple question will help you determine the readiness of the person to accept Jesus as their Lord and Savior.

If a person answers the question by saying, "yes," you will want to be sure to hear their story. Listen carefully to ensure they have heard, believed, and received Jesus as their Lord and Savior. If they have had a true salvation experience, rejoice with them and thank them for allowing you to share. If their story is unclear or something other than a true salvation experience, you may want to ask questions and, in a gentle and kind manner, share with them the difference in your experience and the one you heard them share.

You will want to be sensitive at this point in your witness, but, if all indications are favorable, you may be able to share with the person that what they have told you is something other than the salvation experience the Bible speaks of. You may be able to help them understand the truth. If this goes well, offer them the opportunity to receive Jesus as their Lord and Savior. If a person is resistant to your attempt to clarify the experience they have shared with you, you will want to simply thank them for giving you the opportunity to share what Jesus has done for you and leave the conversation as it is without trying to force the issue. Remember that the Holy Spirit is at work in the whole process and the power of the gospel will continue to work on the one with whom you have been sharing. There is no need to become obnoxious and impolite in a witnessing experience. Leave the door open for another witness to have an opportunity to share their story.

If the person you are witnessing to answers, "No, nothing like that has ever happened to me," you have a wonderful opportunity to share the gospel, the simple gospel, with them. Just follow up the first question ("Has anything like that ever happened to you?") with the question, "Would it be all right if I shared how you can ask Jesus to be the Lord of your life?" If they respond by saying something to the effect that it would not be good at this time, just thank them for listening and leave the door open for another witnessing opportunity. But if they respond by saying that they would like to know how they could ask Jesus to be the Lord of their life proceed to tell them.

Receiving Jesus as Lord requires a personal commitment from every person. Be sure to help the person with whom you are witnessing to voice that commitment to the Lord. You may want to help them with a prayer of commitment. The prayer should be short, simple, and to the point. A sample of this kind of prayer can be as follows:

"Dear Jesus, I want to follow You. I turn from my sin and place my trust in You alone and ask for Your forgiveness. Right now, I receive Your gift of eternal life and confess You as Lord. Thank You for loving me and dying for me. Thank you for giving me new life. In Jesus' name, Amen."

In all likelihood the person will want you to help them voice their commitment to Jesus. Allowing the person to repeat a portion of the prayer after you can do this. You can pray a short portion of the prayer and then pause and allow the person to repeat that portion out loud. Continue with another portion, and another, until the entire prayer of commitment has been completed.

THE MOMENT AFTER

After a person has committed his or her life to Jesus Christ you will want to assure them that the commitment they have just made is real and wonderful. Assure them that God has changed their life whether or not they feel anything. Explain to them that new life in Christ is not a matter of feeling but of faith. A good Bible verse to use is Romans 10:13, "For whoever calls on the name of the Lord shall be saved." If anyone calls on the name of the Lord they are saved whether or not they feel anything because the Bible says so.

Giving a person that has just committed their life to Jesus Christ assurance of their commitment is extremely important. It could make a drastic difference in the life of that new believer. The time you take to share that assurance will pay rich dividends in the life of the new Christian.

You will want to tell the person who has just committed their life to Jesus Christ that their decision was real and wonderful. Tell them that what they have just done is the most important decision of life. Congratulate them for making a great choice.

Chapter 12
"A Plan For Follow Up"

DON'T FALL DOWN–FOLLOW UP

New Christians need the support and fellowship of existing Christians. You will want to do all you can to help those who have committed their life to Jesus get connected with a Bible-believing church in order for them to grow in their faith. The first few weeks after a person has accepted Jesus Christ is a critical time. Just as a newborn baby needs care and love, a new Christian needs the support of a local church.

If the person that has accepted Jesus Christ is a friend of yours, you will want to encourage them to attend church with you. If you do not know the person very well, but know they live in your general area, you will want to see if they want to attend church with you. If the person is not from your area you could ask them if you could contact them with the name and address of a Bible-believing church near them.

Do not neglect this important need in a new believer's life. In other words, don't fall down on follow up. Do all you can to get the new Christian connected to a local, Bible-believing church.

Most Bible-believing churches have a process in place for helping new believers. That process should include a way for the new believer to share with the church the commitment they have made. It should include either some materials or a class that the person can attend to learn more about the decision they have just made. If a church does not have a means of helping new Christians learn more about their new faith you should search for another church that does.

IDENTIFYING WITH CHRIST

There are three important matters that every follow-up process will cover. They are baptism, church membership, and discipleship. Each of these are ways in which new believers identify themselves as a follower of Jesus.

Baptism is one of the identifying marks of a new believer. It is important to understand that in no way does baptism bring about the forgiveness of a person's sins. Receiving new life in Christ is not a matter of being baptized; it is a matter of placing your faith in Jesus; and in Him alone. So the natural question becomes, "Why should a new believer be baptized?"

There are at least two reasons why every believer will want to identify with Christ by being baptized. The first reason is obedience. Baptism demonstrates a willingness to obey what Jesus has commanded. In Matthew 28:19 Jesus told us to, "...baptize them in the name of the Father and of the Son and of the Holy Spirit." If there were no other reason to be baptized other than this first one it should be enough to convince every believer to be baptized.

Baptism is also a public demonstration of a believer's faith. As the new Christians are immersed below the surface of the water, they are demonstrating symbolically that Jesus died and was buried. When the believers are brought up out of the water it demonstrates symbolically that Jesus was raised from the dead.

Baptism symbolically pictures the believer's new life in Christ. Just as Jesus died, was buried, and arose; the new believer too, died to an old way of life and has been raised to new life in Christ. Romans 6:4 says, "Therefore we were buried with Him through baptism into death, that just as Christ was raised from the dead by the glory of the Father, even so, we also should walk in newness of life."

Another identifying mark of a new believer is local church membership. The Bible reveals that new Christians always became a part of the local assembly of believers. The local church is to a new Christian what the home is to a new baby.

It is a place of love, nurture, and training. Without a home a baby would not survive. The same is true of a new believer. It would be a contradiction to be a believer who had no desire to join a local church. Ephesians 5:25 informs us that Christ loves the church and gave Himself for her. We should naturally desire to be a part of that which Jesus Christ loves.

A final identifying mark of believers is discipleship. Discipleship is the term we use to describe the process of learning about and growing in the Lord Jesus. In fact, the word disciple means learner. Discipleship is a life-long process. Jesus commanded in Matthew 28:20 that after baptism comes, "teaching them to observe all things that I have commanded." Believers need to involve themselves in this learning process. The best way to accomplish this command is by involvement in the discipleship process of the local church. Every Bible-believing church will have a process in place to help new believers begin this life-long adventure. If a church does not have a means of discipling believers to observe all that Jesus Christ has commanded you should search for a new church that does.

THERE IS PLENTY OF HELP

We are living in incredible times. The amount of good information available to help us in our efforts to be effective in witnessing is abundant. The appendix includes a list of useful witnessing tools that will assist any Christian. In addition to materials that can be purchased there are a number of good web sites that can be accessed that have a wealth of information that can assist anyone desiring to witness effectively.

Bible-believing churches will be the greatest source of help for witness training. One of the main purposes of the local church and her leaders is to equip Christians in order to observe everything that Jesus Christ has commanded.

Being a witness of the things Jesus Christ has done in our life is the natural result of the transformation that has taken

84

place in every believer. In fact, it is unnatural for a Christian to keep the good news of Jesus Christ to themselves. When the Apostles Peter and John were told that they should not talk about Jesus any more they replied, "... we cannot but speak the things which we have seen and heard." That's how every Christian ought to respond when it comes to being a transformed witness. May it be so that every Christian can not but speak of the things that Jesus Christ has done to transform their life.

APPENDIX 1

Useful Tracts for Witnessing:

"Your Story... How Will It Turn Out"
North American Mission Board, SBC
4200 North Point Pkwy.,
Alpharetta, GA 30022-4176
(800) 448-8032

"Eternal Life"
North American Mission Board, SBC
4200 North Point Pkwy.,
Alpharetta, GA 30022-4176
(800) 448-8032

"Split Time"
North American Mission Board, SBC
4200 North Point Pkwy.,
Alpharetta, GA 30022-4176
(800) 448-8032

"How To Live Forever"
North American Mission Board, SBC
4200 North Point Pkwy.,
Alpharetta, GA 30022-4176
(800) 448-8032

"Between You And God"
American Tract Society
P.O. Box 462008

Garland, TX 75046
(800) 54-TRACT

Witness Training Resource:

The Net: Evangelism for the 21st Century
North American Mission Board, SBC
4200 North Point Pkwy.,
Alpharetta, GA 30022-4176
(800) 448-8032

The Personal Evangelism Training Seminar
www.freshministry.org/pets.htm

Helpful Web Sites for Witnessing:
www.catchthis.net
www.thekristo.com
www.kidzplace.org
www.namb.net
www.theooze.com
www.thefuturechurch.com
www.freshministry.org/postmodern
www.excitement.org/second/thegift.html
www.lifeway.com/24hour/video.htm
www.needhim.org/